SOPHIA'S STORY

SUSAN McKAY

Gill & Macmillan

Gill & Macmillan Ltd
Hume Avenue, Park West, Dublin 12
with associated companies throughout the world
www.gillmacmillan.ie
© Susan McKay 1998, 2004
0 7171 3792 9
Design and print origination by Carole Lynch
Printed and bound by Nørhaven Paperback A/S, Denmark

This book is typeset in 10.5/14.5pt Goudy.

*The paper used in this book comes from the wood pulp of managed
forests. For every tree felled, at least one tree is planted, thereby renewing
natural resources.*

A CIP catalogue record for this book is available from the
British Library.

1 3 5 4 2

DEDICATION

To my daughters, Madeleine and Caitlin,
and to Sophia's son, Gavin

CONTENTS

ACKNOWLEDGMENTS

Thank you, Sophia, for trusting me to write this book, and for working so incredibly hard with me. You faced into the worst of your memories with extraordinary courage and good humour. I am proud that we have become friends.

Thank you, Mike Allen, for your love and support. Thanks also to my parents, Joan and Russell McKay, for all their help, to Madeleine and Caitlin, and to my friend Patsy Brady. Thanks to all the people who gave interviews and information, especially Patsy McColgan and Sally (whose surname cannot be used at the request of relatives). Thanks to all those in Sophia's family who were kind, to Jonathan Williams, and to my colleagues at *The Sunday Tribune*. Finally, thanks to all those who helped but cannot be named.

On Sophia's behalf, thanks and love to her grandparents, Sally and Michael, her mother, Patsy, and her brothers and sisters, Gerry, Keith, Michelle and the younger girls. Her thanks also to Sabina Christensen, Ruth McNeely, Dorothy Morrissey, Ivor Browne, Owen Carthy, James Nugent, Garret Cooney, Chris Meehan, Finola Minch, Detective Sergeant Allo Farragher and his team at Sligo Garda Station, Christina Farrington, all those journalists who reported with sensitivity and respect on the court cases, and all the people who have supported and sustained her over the years.

PREFACE TO THE 2004 EDITION

'For her remarkable courage in exposing the serious deficiencies of a system that failed her and her family, so that others might be spared the suffering she endured.' This was the citation for Sophia McColgan when she was made Irish Person of the Year in 1998, the year *Sophia's Story* was first published. She accepted the honour on behalf of her mother, brothers and sisters. Sophia's brilliant smile lit up the country. Her great spirit touched many people.

The Taoiseach praised this woman who, with her brothers and her sister, had taken the state to court. Government ministers met her to discuss her views on how the victims of child abuse and domestic violence might best be helped. These were the people with the power to change a system that Sophia and her family had proved deficient. They listened, had their photographs taken with her, nodded, promised action.

'All the talk was that what happened to us should never be able to happen in Ireland again,' she says. Six years later, she wonders if very much has changed. 'At the end of our High Court case against the North Western Health Board, the judge said we were all leaving the courtroom sadder but wiser. I'm not sure, though, if Ireland really learned a lot from our story.'

There is no doubt that *Sophia's Story* inspired many people to acts of bravery they had, perhaps, not previously even dared to contemplate. The McColgan siblings proved that the most violent, manipulative and powerful tyrant can be defeated. That his victims can escape and move on to lives in which there is happiness and fulfilment. They also showed that those who collude with abusers can be exposed. That those professionals who are employed to protect the most vulnerable people in society can be made to account for their failure to do so.

The book became a bestseller, and Sophia is proud of the response it received from readers. 'It has been really wonderful the way the story of this family has helped hundreds of others trapped in dysfunctional families to feel that escape is possible from the very worst of situations,' she says. 'We know it has done this because we have had countless letters from other victims. Our hearts go out to all of them. Those who have succeeded, and those who have had setbacks.'

I have also received many letters and phone calls. Some of those who contacted us told how they had been inspired and strengthened by Sophia's courage, to make brave and successful changes in their lives. Others were contemplating such changes, with a mixture of fearfulness and exhilaration.

Other people found that Sophia's honest and unsparing account of her life forced open doors they'd long kept closed. They were no longer able to avoid facing into the damage done to them, or to others they loved, by emotional, physical and sexual abuses such as Sophia describes in her account of her early life. Some told us the book had given them insight into the suicide of someone they cared about.

'No one knows how deep or severe the effects of abuse are,' says Sophia. 'We are all unique and special as individuals. Some people have been traumatised by reading about what happened to me and to my family. Some have ended their lives over just being inappropriately touched. Others have survived extreme abuse.'

Others who made contact were, sadly, people who were too afraid to move, even though their lives were a hell of physical or sexual abuse. These were cries of desolation, but at least represented a start to reaching out for help. Some were people whose experiences of seeking help or seeking justice had been bruising and unsuccessful. Many had huge needs. Sophia, by telling her story, had provided a light that many people dared to hope would see them through dark and scary places.

'This book is a truthful account of my life,' says Sophia. 'But it is also meant to help other people and to encourage them to persist, even if no one seems at first to be listening. It is also meant to make the professionals wake up, and listen. Listen, especially, to what children are telling them.'

Sophia has left Ireland, and lives now in Britain with her partner and their young family. She has trained and qualified as a teacher, and has been given a new perspective on responses to child abuse by this experience. 'I know that awful things can and do happen in the United Kingdom, and that the systems there can also fail people terribly,' she says. 'But it does seem to me that the system in the UK is more capable of being responsive.'

She describes the attitude in schools, for example. 'In Britain, parents are encouraged to come into the classroom, and welcomed. In Ireland, the attitude seems to be that they have no place there and will only be a nuisance. . . . We owe it to our children and to future generations to make school not just a place to learn. It also has the potential to be a place for personal, social and emotional development. Education should prepare children to be strong against abusers in our society.'

She returns to Ireland frequently to visit her family, and has had the experience of trying to help a friend convince a head teacher that a child's allegation about bullying at school should be fully investigated. 'The school had handled the situation in a half-hearted way. The head's attitude was very defensive,' she says. 'I asked to see the school's guidelines on abuse. The advice given was vague. Then I checked the recommended reading, and the report into our case – the West of Ireland farmer case, as it was known – was top of the list! In the UK, there are clear guidelines about who a concerned person should approach if they need to report abuse or suspicions of it.'

Kieran McGrath, an expert in child protection policy, said that in the aftermath of the McColgan case, in 1999, the government introduced new guidelines which demanded higher standards and were good in principle. However, he added: 'In some ways the system is even less effective than before, because the new guidelines are not being implemented.'

There is a crisis in social work, he said, with large numbers of workers leaving, burned out or disillusioned. 'It is commonplace for social work teams to be down forty per cent on their complement,' he said. 'People are struggling to provide a basic service.

'You have children on long waiting lists to be assessed in cases of suspected abuse. You have difficult cases being allocated to inexperienced workers just out of college. You have homeless children being managed on a crisis basis by duty social workers. You have children in care who don't have an allocated social worker. No one could say it is good practice.'

In one respect, Sophia says, Ireland has services that are better than those she has found to be available in the UK. 'Our Rape Crisis Centres and Women's Aid services are brilliant,' she says. When she first met Dorothy Morrissey of the Limerick Rape Crisis Centre in 1993, she said, 'for the first time in my life I found somebody who believed me and who understood.'

'Phenomenal' is the word chosen by Fiona Neary, the co-ordinator of the Network of Rape Crisis Centres, to describe the impact Sophia, and *Sophia's Story*, have had on raising awareness about rape, child abuse and domestic violence in the family. 'We owe her a great debt,' she says. 'Unfortunately, Rape Crisis Centres are so grossly underfunded that we can't cope with the demand for our services.' Most centres have waiting lists of several months, and some don't advertise because they don't want to disappoint. The Dublin Rape Crisis Centre periodically has to close down its waiting lists.

The Sexual Assault and Violence in Ireland report of 2002 showed a huge incidence of sexual violence. It revealed that half of those who had been abused didn't disclose it, and that most didn't contact any support agency. Out of those who go to Rape Crisis Centres, just twenty per cent will report to the Gardaí. Other studies show that only one per cent of those reported will result in a conviction – the lowest rate out of twenty-one EU countries. 'As a country, we have a long way to go,' says Neary.

Sophia's mother, Patsy, tried to escape from Joseph McColgan with her children back in 1979, but felt there was nowhere she could go. Although there is now a network of Women's Aid refuges, according to Rachel Mullen of Women's Aid, the numbers of women fleeing violent men is constantly increasing, and there is still nowhere to go for too many women.

'In 1999, in the Eastern Region, two out of every three women seeking a space in a refuge were refused,' she says. 'The housing shortage is even more acute now, so the situation is actually getting worse.' She also says that legal protections for women and children are still 'totally inadequate', and that there was a 'lack of commitment' to the regional steering committees set up to work towards preparing a strategic plan on tackling domestic violence and rape.

The statute of limitations over which the McColgans had to

struggle with the state remains in place for cases of physical abuse, though the government was forced to lift it temporarily in cases of sexual abuse in 1999. This was because the McColgan case was followed by the revelations in Mary Raftery's *States of Fear* documentary into institutional abuse. The Taoiseach apologised to victims of child sexual abuse, set up the Laffoy Tribunal and then denied Miss Justice Laffoy the co-operation and the funding she needed. She resigned in protest.

We now have our first Ombudsman for children, appointed in 2003, but her budget is tiny compared with that provided for the equivalent office in the North, which has a much smaller population.

For his horrific crimes, Joseph McColgan was given a cumulative total of 238 years in prison, the longest in Irish legal history. He was directed to serve them concurrently, meaning he was sentenced to twelve years. With remission, he is to be released this year, 2004. His name will go on the register of sex offenders, a measure described by McGrath as 'weak'.

'He has no power over me any more,' says Sophia. 'I do not fear him. But this is a man who almost murdered children. We, his family, know how dangerous he is. I just hope others do as well.'

Susan McKay
January 2004

'Honour thy father and thy mother.'

'It was a beautiful sunny day. The sun was pouring through the leaves, sparkling off the leaves. I can see it. It was up in the woods at Derreen Bog. His face was above me. He threw me on the ground. All I remember is the pain. Excruciating pain. I was bleeding. There was slimy stuff.

When we got home, he said, "Sophia saw frogspawn in the woods today and she didn't know what it was." Everyone laughed. I suppose he really wanted to get me under his grip of fear quickly and that he did very effectively and in a most cruel manner. It was so horrific to me that I was petrified. I couldn't talk.

That was a short while before I made my First Holy Communion. I was very shocked and confused. Distraught really. In preparation, we had been taught, "Honour thy father and thy mother." We were taught that we should love and adore them. I loved my parents. Well, I loved my mother anyway. I thought I would be a bad girl if I hated my father.

I remember going into the chapel. There was a moment to make a prayer for the future. I wished and wished that this would end and I could be happy. I was six.'

INTRODUCTION

On 4 December 1997, Senior Counsel James Nugent stood up in Court Number One in Dublin's Four Courts and addressed Mr Justice Johnson and the High Court:

My Lord, Sophia McColgan is now twenty-seven years of age. She is a laboratory technician and she is the mother of a son. She has a relationship with the father of her son. The fact that she is all of that is a remarkable feat, because between the years of 1978 and the end of the Eighties or the start of the Nineties, she was the subject of a sustained savage and brutal assault, both physical and sexual, by her father. The details of it are horrific . . .

The case is, of course, not against her father, Joseph McColgan, because he was tried for the offences and he pleaded guilty to twenty-six token charges and he is currently in jail. The case is against the North Western Health Board and against the general practitioner, Dr Moran . . .

Sophia is the second of six children. Her elder brother Gerard, herself and her younger sister Michelle were born in England and were sent home to Sligo to live with their maternal grandparents. For the first few years of their lives they had a happy and balanced existence, but from the time their parents came home from England and went to look after their children, their lives turned into a living hell. This was the mid-Seventies. This was at a time when there was significant publicity in the UK and in this country on child abuse. The Department of Health here was circulating the health boards with guidelines as to how suspected cases of child abuse might be dealt with . . .

Mr Nugent went on to describe how Sophia had been sent to Sligo General Hospital after 'she had clearly been physically abused'. The doctor who referred her, Dr Doreen Dunleavy, described her as a 'battered child'. Mr Nugent said that Sophia's mother, Patsy McColgan, had told the people in the Health Board that her husband was physically abusive not just to Sophia, but to her other daughter, Michelle, her son Gerry, and herself.

The authorities seemed to hold case conferences. Sophia was held in hospital until the end of August 1979 and then she was returned home. There seems to have been vague good intentions, vague worry . . . When she went home, Sophia and her mother were subjected to horrendous physical abuse. Sophia at this stage was a nine-year-old girl and it had the effect of silencing her for a very long time.

Mr Nugent described how Gerry, then ten, was soon afterwards sent to Sligo Hospital by the same doctor, who once again used the words 'battered child' in her note of referral. There was another case conference. 'I am not saying people were not concerned,' said Mr Nugent. He said, however, that they did not act effectively: 'Gerry was returned to the family home and savagely assaulted.' Mr

Nugent described a series of communications between doctors and psychiatrists, culminating in a plan that the whole family was to be seen by a child guidance clinic. 'Mr McColgan, who was known at this stage to be a violent, abusive man, would not agree to that and therefore it was dropped as an idea. Instead there was a second case conference,' Mr Nugent said. At this conference, Dr Moran described Gerry as a manipulative boy. (Dr Moran said after the court case that his comment had been taken out of context.) He and the public health nurse were given responsibility for monitoring the family, but there appeared to be little communication between Dr Moran and the Health Board arising from that. Mr Nugent then said that as well as the physical violence, the children were being sexually abused, though this was not revealed at this stage to any of the health professionals. At this time, one thousand copies of the Department of Health's guidelines were sent to the North Western Health Board (NWHB).

Mr Nugent said that by this time, Patsy McColgan had been battered into silence. 'The unfortunate Mrs McColgan had literally been beaten out of the picture. She said whatever her husband wanted her to say . . . although she was physically present, she had just opted out. 'It is not something anyone could condemn her for, as she lived a life of hell.' Mr Nugent spoke about Gerry's admission to hospital in 1981 with a broken arm. A failed court case followed, at which no information appears to have been presented about previous acts of violence. 'Nothing happened. Nothing was done. There was no effort to take the children into care.' Mr Nugent went on to describe the violence which had led to Gerry running away and being taken into care. At a case conference, Dr Moran said he would not recommend the 'soft option'; what the boy needed was 'hard discipline'. In care, Gerry disclosed that he and Sophia had been sexually abused. 'He gave them graphic details of what happened,' said Mr Nugent. 'Someone suggested Sophia should be looked at. Dr Moran suggested it to the mother and she told the father immediately and any such examination was refused by them. Again, nothing was done.' (Dr Moran's Counsel would tell the court that this examination did take place.)

Mr Nugent then read from a report written in April 1984 by social worker Val O'Kelly, who described 'a pathological family' within which 'the degree of abuse both physical and sexual is at an extraordinary level'. She said that in the family, 'abuse is the norm' and that Mrs McColgan colluded with her husband in the violence 'to the detriment of their children'. She described Joseph McColgan as 'very sick' and 'seriously perverted'. Ms O'Kelly added that Sophia should be spoken to.

It might be expected, commented Mr Nugent, that after such a report, something would be done. 'Something was done,' he said. It appeared that, after consideration, the file on the family was closed. He said Gerry left care, lived with his maternal grandparents for a time, and then went to England to try to build a life. 'Sophia, Michelle and Keith were left. The abuse went on and on and on, year in, year out. Not a finger was raised to help them. Sophia as she grew older began to stand up for herself, but as she resisted her father's perverse attentions, Michelle and Keith came into the firing line.'

Mr Nugent said that by 1991, when Sophia left home, 'The father must by this stage have felt that he was untouchable.' However, he said, after an incident in which he ran Michelle down with his motorbike, she told a friend and the friend brought her to Dr Jane Dorman, a Sligo GP. The doctor contacted social workers, who contacted the Gardaí. 'After that, events moved quickly. The father was charged with a litany of horrendous offences with physical and sexual abuse,' Mr Nugent said. 'Obviously it seems clear from a recitation of the facts what the case against both the Health Board and Dr Moran is. A reply, by way of defence, my Lord, is, in the circumstances of this case, staggering.'

Mr Nugent said the NWHB was claiming that there was no statable cause of action, that the action was barred by the provisions of the Statute of Limitations, and that it was not negligent. The Board was also claiming that there was contributory negligence on the part of Sophia.

'The defence of Dr Moran is even more extraordinary in that they deny, or do not admit, notwithstanding that ultimately the father pleaded guilty to these offences — they do not admit that Sophia was ever assaulted physically or sexually,' Mr Nugent said. Dr Moran denied negligence, and said that the plaintiff had failed to inform her mother that she was being sexually assaulted and abused and that she had failed to inform the Gardaí.

'On the question of how all this affected Sophia, I think the coward in me would like to tell your Lordship that you could just go to the end of the scale and mark this down as a little bit worse because then we would not have to consider what was done and what the effect of it was. I don't think that form of hiding is open to me.' He went on to say that from around the time of Sophia's First Holy Communion, when her teachers were telling her to 'love, honour and particularly obey' her parents, her father was subjecting her to repeated sexual and physical assaults. Mr Nugent said he would not go into graphic detail. It would suffice to say that, 'every orifice of her body was invaded'.

In the hushed courtroom, many people were in tears. Mr Nugent was himself visibly moved. 'How she coped with that, I suppose no one will ever know.' He told Mr Justice Johnson that, as a result of what had happened, Sophia and her family did not trust people. 'They do not trust your Lordship, they do not trust me and they do not trust their solicitor. They do not really trust anyone. For any trust they should have had was betrayed.'

Mr Nugent concluded by telling the judge that he might be surprised to learn that he would not be asking him to instruct the media to protect Sophia's anonymity. The family had decided to go public. The 'West of Ireland Farmer', as Sophia's father had been dubbed in media reports of his trial in the criminal courts in 1995, was Joseph McColgan. The health professionals were the North Western Health Board and Dr Desmond Moran, the county coroner.

Sophia had nothing to hide. Her days of silence were over. She and her family had got her father jailed; now they needed to know why the professional people they believed could have helped them when they were children in need, had so obviously not done so.

The case which followed lasted thirteen long days, spread over eight long weeks. Every aspect of Sophia's life was exposed, including her most intimate relationships. She sat, day after day, on the public benches of Court One, where she had sat during the criminal trial of her father two years previously. She spent two days in the witness box. 'I did get very angry and frustrated sometimes, because I wanted to get it across that this was a child they were talking about, a child whose father was a monster,' she said. 'But cross-examination was nothing compared with the kind of interrogations my father used to put me through. I was not afraid. I knew I was telling the truth.'

However, it was a stressful time, and it had its bizarre moments. Sophia was staying in a bed and breakfast not far from the courts. One night, she was woken by a crash, to find that part of the ceiling of her room had cracked from end to end. The landlady explained to her anxious guests that the wall of Arbour Hill prison next door had collapsed in the night. 'I hadn't known we were even near the prison,' said Sophia. (Joseph McColgan was initially held at Arbour Hill but has since been transferred to the Curragh prison in Co. Kildare.) And there were bright moments. Another day a bunch of yellow roses arrived from the women who run the Wexford Rape Crisis Centre. At weekends, Sophia would go home to her child who would jump into her arms for the happiness of seeing his mother.

At one stage of the proceedings, Sophia rejected an offer of £250,000, offered on condition that she settle the case there and then. The catch was that there would be just £40,000 each for her siblings. 'I didn't yield,' she said. 'I thought of my Great-Granny, my mother's Granny, and I knew she would say, "Go in there and fight for your brothers and sister."' So she did.

The intensive media interest in the case was daunting. Some of the reporting was, as in the criminal case, salacious. However, mostly Sophia was glad that the reporters were there. 'I got dozens of cards and letters at Christmas, and so did my brothers and sister, from people all over the country,' she said. 'It was nice to know that people cared.' There are cards from people who were themselves abused, including some from survivors of brutality at Goldenbridge Orphanage (children in care at this Dublin home, run by Sisters of Mercy, were cruelly maltreated from the 1930s to the Seventies). There are cards from mothers. There are many, many cards from people telling Sophia that she was one of the bravest people they had ever seen and that they were hoping and praying that she would get justice at last. One man sent a message of support through journalist Carole Coulter of *The Irish Times*. His wife had been a victim of child abuse and had committed suicide.

It was perhaps Dr Alice Swann who summed up best why people were so enthralled and moved by Sophia.

She is exceptional. In all my years of working with children, young people and adults who have been abused, there are, in my mind, three or four cases where the person has given all of us a window into what the world of the abused child is like, and she is one such person. There are very few that actually give you that window. Many give you glimpses, but very few actually have the capacity to show you exactly what it is like. I think we have to learn from her and her like.

On 23 January 1998 it ended. Senior Counsel Garret Cooney told Mr Justice Johnson that the case had been settled, adding that there had been no admission of liability by either the NWHB or Dr Moran. Mr Justice Johnson briefly addressed the court before he rose. He said he was delighted that the case was settled. 'We cannot but leave this court sadder and wiser,' he said. Sophia remained in the now quiet courtroom for a time, writing thank-you cards to her solicitor, Owen Carthy of Kevin Kilraine and Company, her barristers, James Nugent, Garret Cooney and Chris Meehan, and the judge, Mr Justice Johnson.

A short time later, she and her brothers, Gerry and Keith, pushed open the doors of the Four Courts and emerged, blinking in the winter sunlight, into a scrum of press photographers and reporters. Sophia and her family smiled and smiled and smiled. Then she read from a brief statement they had prepared together.

The settlement of these proceedings has resulted in the payment to each of us of a substantial six figure sum for damages, together with the payment of all our legal costs. We believe we have told the truth, that we have been listened to, and that justice has been done. We are very grateful to the very many people who have offered their support to us throughout the duration of the case. This was a source of great comfort to us. It is our earnest wish that this case will help other people who have been the victims of abuse to realise that there is no shame in having been abused.

This is Sophia's story.

1

'WHAT'S ALL THE FUSS ABOUT?'

⁂

It was good fun in the hospital. There were lots of other little children in the ward, and, after a day or two, Sophia relaxed. They played and played, the children. The nurses would come round with the medicine trolley and the children would cluster around, as if it was a mobile sweet shop. It was warm, there were toys, there was food, and you could sleep at night. Sophia had a nice new nightdress that her Granny Sally had bought her in Sligo. It was pink with a lacy neck. When anyone asked, 'What happened to your nose?' she replied, 'My father hit me.' She told the doctors, the nurses, the visitors, the children. It was so simple. She was safe at last.

Sophia, then aged nine, had taken a huge risk. Her father had warned her that if she told on him, he would kill her. She had told on him. There was no going back. It happened on 25 July 1979. The middle of the International Year of the Child. The year the Pope came to Ireland. Nineteen years later, she remembers that terrifying morning.

We were up in Granny's house and he ordered me to come down to the cottage with him. I knew in my heart and soul he was going to rape me because he was isolating me from the others. I was sick of the way he was abusing me and the way he was treating us. I decided in my mind I had had enough. I'd seen my brother Gerry running away and telling everyone about the beatings we were getting. I'd seen Gerry brought home time and again. Then he'd get ferocious beatings. He was made an example of, to terrify the rest of us.

I had made my mind up to defy my father on a particular occasion when there were other people present. I thought that if I came up with something to show what was happening to me too, then it would prove Gerry was telling the truth and they would help us and we would be saved.

That day, we were in Granny's and I knew she'd do her best. I really trusted her to save me. I decided to defy him. I said, 'No.' I refused to go to the cottage. I refused to be raped. He just took me into this small bedroom and he locked the door and he beat me stupid. He thumped me and kicked me. I was like a ragdoll being belted and thumped around this room. I remember my ears were really ringing. I couldn't hear anything. In the end he pushed me and I hit my nose on the handle of the door.

Sally, Sophia's maternal grandmother, remembers that day vividly. She was serving in her small grocery shop beside her home at the top of Ballinacarrow village, a brief straggle of houses with a chapel at one end and a school at the other, situated on a slope in the road twelve miles from Sligo on the road to Galway. Sophia's grandfather, Michael, a sacristan at the local chapel, was away on a pilgrimage to Lough Derg. It was pension day, and a few neighbours were in the shop for their messages. Sally was giving one of them, Joe Langan, his change, when her daughter Patsy threw open the door. Patsy, her husband Joe McColgan and their children, Gerry (ten), Sophia (nine), Michelle (seven) and Keith (four), were staying with Sally and Michael while they renovated the old cottage a mile and a half down the road, to which they were planning to move.

When Patsy burst into the shop, she was shouting for help and crying. 'She said, "Come quick, he's got Sophia in the back bedroom and he's killing her,"' recalled Sally. 'There were some of the neighbours in the shop. One of them was Evelyn McBrien, God rest her, a teacher. She was there. She said she'd come with me, because she knew I wouldn't be able to cope on my own. Joe Langan came as well, a very honest and decent man.'

Miss McBrien was a prominent person in the small village of Ballinacarrow. Her house was a place where people gathered to *ceili*, have a drink and a talk. Patsy McColgan went there as a child to watch 'The Fugitive' on TV, or to dress up in the kindly teacher's high heels and dresses.

'Evelyn McBrien shouted in for Joe McColgan to open the door. We could hear Sophia screaming and crying. Then a neighbour man shouted in at him, "Let out that child or I'll kick the door down." Next of all, we heard the door opening and Joe McColgan stuck his head out and said, as cool as anything, "What's all the fuss about? There's nothing wrong here." Then we saw Sophia. There was blood all over her face and she was crying. Gerry ran off about a mile down the road to get my brother, because we didn't know what Joe McColgan would do next,' said Sally. 'Evelyn McBrien ran down the road and rang the Gardaí. They were here within ten minutes. She rang Dr Dunleavy too. After we brought Sophia in to clean up her face at the next-door neighbour's, we knew she was badly hurt.'

McColgan strode out past his injured daughter, got onto his tractor and ordered the children up. Patsy pulled Michelle and Keith back. Joe Langan remonstrated with McColgan, who told him to mind his own business, because, he said, 'This is a family matter.' Cursing them all, McColgan then took off on his own. Patsy spoke with the Gardaí in her mother's kitchen. She shakes her head at the memory of that day nearly twenty years ago. 'A Garda told me I could sign him into the mental hospital, but he could be out in three days,' she said. She left the house, distraught.

When the doctor, Doreen Dunleavy, arrived she found Sophia in a terrified state. 'She said, "I'm afraid this child seems to have a broken nose; you'll have to take her to hospital,"' said Sally. Dr Dunleavy, who did not know the family and had never met Sophia, questioned Sally and made a swift assessment of the situation. She scribbled a note for the admitting staff at casualty: 'Please see this battered child. Beaten by father this a.m. while in a raged state. He does not drink. Took child to sitting room, caught her neck with his hands, locked the door. This history has been related to me by wife's mother. The parents have been married ten years, have four children. Lived in England . . . came home to Ballinacarrow, building a home there. The four kids have been beaten many times as has his wife. Observed and examined very frightened child, obvious injury to nasal bone. Bruising under upper lip . . . this family would need to be seen by a social worker.' Dr Dunleavy would later phone the hospital to reinforce her concern, and her husband, also a doctor, would contact the North Western Health Board.

Joe Langan took Sophia and her grandmother to the General Hospital in Sligo. As they passed the gloomy roadside cottage to which her father had demanded she accompany him that morning, and to which he intended them to move permanently,

Sophia pressed her bloodied bandage to her face and dared to think, 'Never again'.

There was much that nine-year-old Sophia did not know about events in her family during those few days in the summer of 1979. She did not know that the night before she resolved to stand up to her father, her mother had also decided she could not take any more. Speaking to me in 1998, Patsy said, 'The physical and mental abuse was awful.' She ran her finger along her nose. 'He gave me a broken nose too one time.' That night in 1979, the family was down working at the wretched cottage. Its squalor was proving resistant to the hard labour that had gone into it. Patsy had, by this time, four children under the age of ten, and was pregnant again. She cannot remember what the particular act of violence was that precipitated it, but she left the house and thumbed a lift into Sligo. She went to the home of her husband's mother and asked for help.

The late Mrs McColgan senior was a stern and forbidding person. She disapproved of Patsy and encouraged her son to regard her as an unfit mother for his children. The McColgan parents of Circular Road, Sligo saw themselves as a family of consequence. McColgan senior was a rate collector, and latterly a lollipop man at a local school. Circular Road would be known, in class-conscious Sligo, as 'a good address'. The McColgan parents looked down on Joseph, who had palpably not come to much. 'There was a terrible lack of love,' Patsy said.

Joe McColgan's parents encouraged him to blame his problems with the children on Patsy and her parents. 'They thought I was an unfit mother because I gave my three eldest children to my mother to rear while we were in England,' said Patsy. 'They blamed me. I had created them.' Patsy said her husband often told her that it would be better for everyone if she died, since he was the only fit parent in the family. The children had often heard

Grandmother McColgan say, 'Spare the rod and spoil the child.' Sophia remembers journeys in Grandfather McColgan's old Volkswagen, when he would make the children repeat incessantly, 'Blessed Lord Jesus, grant us eternal rest . . .'

That night, Joe McColgan's parents drove Patsy back to the cottage at Cloonacurra. There they collected the children, who were locked out and had been standing in the field beside the house, waiting. They drove their son's family to Sally and Michael's house, where everyone sat down to await McColgan's return. 'But when he came in, they just sat there like zombies and said nothing to him,' said Patsy. The following morning, McColgan went off at 6.00 a.m., returning 'in a foul mood' at 9.00. That was when he demanded of Sophia that she accompany him to the cottage. That was when Sophia said, 'No.'

It was nineteen years later, on 21 December 1997, in the High Court in Dublin, when Sophia learned something else about that brutal day in 1979. Garret Cooney, along with James Nugent, was Sophia's Counsel in the damages case against the North Western Health Board and GP Dr Desmond Moran. During examination by Mr Cooney, social worker Edna Keown was asked to read from a summary she had compiled of contacts between the Board and the McColgan family. She said that the summary had been compiled as part of a training exercise. Ms Keown revealed that when on 24 July 1979 Patsy McColgan had left the house after her husband had beaten up Sophia, Patsy had herself gone to Sligo. She went first to her mother-in-law, Mrs McColgan. The two women then went together to the offices of Sligo Social Services, a voluntary organisation run by the Catholic Church. Patsy told Sister Áine there that her husband was beating her and the children. 'Take the children into care,' Patsy said. 'They are not safe with him.'

Patsy McColgan has a pale, mask-like face, a face used to gripping its expression in, keeping back emotion. During the damages case, to which she had been brought under subpoena by the NWHB, she sat with her now adult sons and daughters, Gerry and Keith, Sophia and Michelle, on the public benches. When Ms Keown made this revelation, Patsy looked as if she had been turned to stone. Months later, sitting in Patsy's kitchen in the house she rents in a small town in County Sligo, mother and daughter spoke to me about this emotionally charged information. 'We never knew,' said Sophia. 'That day in court was the first time we had ever heard it.'

'I thought I'd die when all that was said in court,' said Patsy. 'I was absolutely devastated. I thought the kids would think I had wanted to get rid of them.' Sophia, listening to her mother, shook her head. 'No, Mammy. That's not how I see it at all,' she said, gently. 'You were trying to protect us. You've no need to feel guilty about that.' 'I don't know,' said Patsy, miserable, unconvinced. It was one of the threats her husband had used down the years: that if anyone told about the things that went on in his house, the family would be split up, the children put in separate homes and none of them would see each other ever again. 'He used to tell the kids, "If your mother has her way, you'll be put in homes,"' said Patsy.

Patsy was completely distraught when she spoke to Sister Áine in Sligo. The nun, seeing that this was a serious matter, referred her to Markievicz House. She was brought there by social worker Deirdre Taheny. Then the headquarters of the community care team in Sligo, Markievicz House is a big, dilapidated white house with black-framed windows, overlooking the harbour. When she arrived there, with her mother-in-law, Patsy was so distressed she could hardly speak. In a meeting with Ms Taheny and senior social worker Denis Duffy, she repeated that she wanted her children taken into care for their safety. Mr Duffy had just learned that Sophia had been admitted to hospital.

The social worker noted that Patsy said her husband had beaten Sophia, and had described him as 'easily angered'. She told them that, while he seemed to have some regard for the youngest child, Keith, he was 'particularly violent' towards their oldest son, Gerry. Patsy believes she was 'lenient' in the way she described her husband to the social workers. 'I thought I was to blame, for sending the children home to my parents,' she said. 'He had me convinced of that.'

Adopting her husband's version of their troubles, Patsy explained to the social workers that the three oldest children had been brought up by her parents while she and her husband were working in England, and that he resented their interference. She said he tried to keep the children away from their grandparents by bringing them down to the cottage during the day. Mr Duffy suggested that it might be better to consider care for Sophia only, since he believed this could be justified on the basis of the evidence. Ms Taheny's record of the meeting stated that the view was taken that to remove all the children 'would give Mr McColgan reason to complain and he had parental rights to his children which could not be overlooked'.

Patsy signed a reception-into-care form on behalf of Sophia. After discussion, she said the other children would be safe at home in her parents' house, because her husband had left and was unlikely to return. The social workers decided that on discharge from hospital, Sophia could go to Nazareth House, a residential care centre run by nuns with a unit subsidised by the NWHB. A place was reserved for her there.

Denis Duffy, who had worked in social services in Britain before returning to the north-west of Ireland, retired in 1990. He spoke to me in a personal capacity and apologised for the fact that some of his recollections of his contacts with the McColgan family are confused. 'It was nineteen years ago, don't forget,' he said. His recollection of the meeting with Patsy McColgan was that she was distressed and almost mute throughout, while her mother-in-law talked incessantly. 'Mrs McColgan senior kept going on about how Joe had got too big for his boots and needed to be taught a lesson, that he had to grow up,' said Mr Duffy. 'None of what was said implied serious wrongdoing. All I gathered was that he was capable of making people unhappy, that there had been a major husband and wife row and that he had hit or caused Sophia some distress.'

McColgan stayed away that night, at his parents' house in town. The following day, Patsy was brought to visit Sophia in hospital. The child had slept well and seemed content. Dr Brian McDonagh, a paediatrician, had examined her nose and found that it was fractured but not broken. He took photographs of her facial injuries. She looks out of the photographs with her big deep eyes, one of them bruised, a swollen nose, and a wide, shy smile revealing a cut lip.

After leaving Sophia at the hospital, Patsy McColgan was brought by social workers to see a solicitor. The Health Board records note that she was advised about barring orders and legal separation. Ms Keown read from her summary of contacts with the McColgans that the solicitor had advised Mrs McColgan that, 'Separation would involve taking the case to the High Court and would be very expensive.' On barring orders, the advice was, as interpreted in the social work record, 'The difficulty with a barring order is that it must be renewed every three months.'

Looking back, Patsy feels that she needed a lot more information about her options, if she had any. 'I got legal advice but all I could hear was that it would be expensive to get away from him,' she recalled. 'I felt, rightly or wrongly, it was being put over to me that I couldn't afford it. I couldn't even afford to put food on the table. Once I heard that money was involved, that was it. I had four children under the age of ten and I was expecting another. I had no idea if I was entitled to anything, or how I'd manage if I was able to get a job.'

During this crisis, while Sophia was in hospital, Patsy stayed at her mother's house with the other children. Her husband did not attempt to physically abuse his family, but he did keep up the mental pressure. Sally said McColgan used to drive up to the wall at the front of the house several times a day. 'He'd arrive at the gate and call her out,' she said. Patsy said she was in mental turmoil. 'I was incapable of making a decision.' Sally said that, at the time, she wanted her daughter to leave Joseph McColgan. Although she is religious, and her husband is a particularly devout Catholic, she said she urged Patsy to stay with her, get a job, and she would mind the children. 'Even the nuns who taught me growing up, said that what you thought was right is your duty,' she said. 'It is your duty to know that no one belonging to you is abused.'

McColgan had other plans, though. While his wife agonised and Sophia played contentedly in the hospital, he launched himself on the Health Board. On 27 July, he turned up at Markievicz House in a fury. His mother was with him. Mr Duffy remembers his first meeting with McColgan. 'He was a most arrogant, unpleasant man,' he said. 'He traipsed around my office, towering over my desk. He said there was no air in the place and opened the window — all the symptoms of someone who has to dominate every space. There was simply no way to get through to him. His mother appeared to be afraid of him.'

In the course of a three-hour meeting, McColgan shouted his mother down, and raised his voice when any of those present dared to voice an opinion. 'He was dressed to kill and bragged about how many suits he had,' Mr Duffy recalled. 'I would say he was as cunning as hell, but not mad. It was apparent that he was a bully.' McColgan claimed at the meeting that he had been victimised and that no one had asked him for his version of the story of how Sophia had got hurt. He claimed that he had merely pushed her after she had disobeyed him, and that she had then tripped and accidentally banged her nose against the door. He said his wife had exaggerated the incident.

McColgan said that the root of the problem was that he and his family had no privacy because they were forced to live with his parents-in-law. He said the children disobeyed him and had no respect for him, loving their grandparents more than him. He informed social workers that he was a believer in 'strict discipline' and 'punishment' for disobedience. It was clear to them that he included his wife in this required obedience.

Ms Taheny, who had visited Sophia in hospital the previous day and had noted that the child was 'extremely frightened', observed that the little girl's father appeared 'very domineering, with an archaic view of the father's role in the household'. He told her that the more he tried to get the children to respect him, the more they ignored him and turned to their grandparents. His only wish, he said, was 'to reunite the family' as a separate unit away from their relations. He was advised to meet his wife, possibly at Markievicz House. Ms Taheny noted that he had agreed to do so 'to discuss their difficulties with a view to some reconciliation'.

Sophia, playing contentedly in the children's ward less than a mile away, thought she had seen the last of her father. However, towards the end of the meeting between McColgan and the social workers, Mr Duffy had another suggestion for the angry man before him. Mr Duffy advised McColgan to go to the hospital and visit Sophia. I asked him, at our meeting in 1998, why he had done so. Mr Duffy said, 'Because, in the first place, he ought to be making up to the child for his misdemeanour.' Had McColgan shown any signs of remorse? 'No way,' said Mr Duffy. 'He was as white as the driven snow in his eyes.' The visit was not supervised because, Mr Duffy said, 'a father has the right to visit his child. We couldn't interfere in that.'

They said to me, 'You have a visitor,' said Sophia. 'It was about a week and a half or two weeks into my time in the hospital. I looked around and saw him. I froze. You know, I had temporarily forgotten that he existed. All I wanted was to go back to Granny and my mother and brothers and sister. I thought that all the people would see that my father was completely deranged and that he wouldn't get a chance to come anywhere near us again. I had prayed for that at mass in the hospital. When he came into the ward, I started to sweat and shake. The fear hit me.

He took his time coming over to me. He talked to all the little girls in the ward. He got to know them all while I was in there. There was one little girl — she had the same nightdress as me — and he was talking to her. She innocently said to him, 'Why did you break Sophia's nose?' 'What did you say?' he said. 'Sophia says you hit her and broke her nose,' she said. I was listening and I was terrified, but I still thought it would be all right because I was thinking about my Granny and Dr Dunleavy and all the doctors and nurses who knew. I thought, 'Look at all the people who can help me now.' My father listened to the little girl telling him this, and he said, 'You're a very good girl for telling me that, now. That's not true at all.' And she laughed. The little girl laughed and put her hand over her mouth, and she said, 'Oh! Sophia's been telling lies!'

She believed him. I felt really, really terrible about that. It is very hard to describe that feeling. It is that he was making up that I'd said something wrong and I knew I'd said something right, but she believed him. He would always say I was telling lies, when I knew I was telling the truth, and he'd laugh about it. That day in the hospital, I felt so undermined. I felt like a really bad girl. I felt guilty for telling the truth. He made me feel very bad for telling the truth, and he made me feel I was a spiteful little girl for telling the truth.

McColgan came over to his child where she was standing petrified and drained of strength at the side of her bed. 'I thought he was going to hit me there and then,' said Sophia. 'Now, aren't you very bad to be telling lies about your daddy?' he said. 'We'll have to see what we'll do about that when we get you home.' Then he handed her the book he had brought in for her. 'He never gave me presents. It was just to make him look good in front of the nurses and doctors,' said Sophia. 'He was wearing his suit that day too. I remember the book was called *My First Dictionary*. There were pictures of animals in it. It was a book for a five-year old and I was nine. He had written on the inside of it, "To Sophia, my darling daughter, love from Daddy."' Sophia told me that she had looked in silent horror at the inscription. 'I had never known this Daddy,' she said.

The campaign of attrition against Patsy was also continuing. McColgan enlisted a priest to go and speak to his wife. Patsy remembers the interview well. 'The priest kind of said it was a shame to be thinking of leaving my marriage after ten years. He said marriage was for life and women had to put up with certain things. He reminded me of the vows. "Till death us do part." He said I should try to compromise,' she said. 'He said I should make it up with my husband and have another go at making my marriage work.' Patsy listened. She had been brought up in a warm and loving home with strong Catholic values. There is a statue of the Blessed Virgin in front of the house where Sally and Michael raised their four daughters. Although her mother was now telling her she didn't have to go back to her husband, the old authority of the priest swayed her. 'I did feel I had a duty to try again to make my marriage work,' she said. 'Then again, where do you go with five children and no money in this country? I thought he might change. I must have been awful stupid. It was the biggest mistake of my life.'

Sophia's sense of safety in the hospital was dissipating rapidly. Her parents now came together to visit her. Her grandmother, Sally, still visited, even though it was hard for her to get away from the shop and travel into town by bus. Her husband had a lot of church duties at this time. 'One day I went in and they said, "She already has a visitor,"' recalled Sally. 'It was Joe McColgan. After that I couldn't stay with Sophia or he'd raise a riot.' Patsy and Joe McColgan also attended a psychiatrist at St Columba's Hospital, and had several meetings with Dr McDonagh. The plan was that they would attempt to get the Cloonacurra cottage ready to live in quickly. McColgan's view that what they needed was to get away from Patsy's parents and sort out their problems in private was now the predominant one, accepted by Patsy. Although Sophia did not know it, while the place at Nazareth House was still available, she was now only being kept in hospital until the NWHB authorities were satisfied that the situation at home had eased and that her parents had become reconciled.

On 10 August, her parents visited her in hospital. Ms Taheny noted that the couple seemed amicable, and that Patsy was disappointed that Sophia was not to be let home straight away. McColgan, on the other hand, said it was better if she stayed there for the moment. In retrospect, it is clear that McColgan did not want Sophia to get back to her grandparents. Mr Duffy said that from the records he would say that Patsy, who had been almost mute during his meeting with her in July, was by this stage 'more like a wife and mother'.

What Sophia did not tell anyone in the hospital was that her father was not just beating her. 'By then he was raping me, in the house, in the shed, in the field, after mass on a Sunday, when he'd bring me home ahead of the others and molest me before my mother got home. It was whenever he got the opportunity. He had affected me psychologically so badly, I was so terrified, that I was ashamed and embarrassed to tell anyone he was sexually abusing me.' During the 1998 damages case, she told her Counsel, James Nugent, of her memories of blinding pain. 'I thought that I would never get through it or through my life.'

Mr Nugent asked her in the court why she had not revealed any of this while she was in hospital. 'I wasn't able to,' she replied. 'Nobody gave me the space or the time. Nobody took me in hand and asked me was this what was happening in the home. I felt that I could have told somebody if they had given me the opportunity to tell them, if they had given me space when my father wasn't there. I would say it would have taken me a few weeks to get enough trust and confidence to tell anyone.'

Cross-examined on this by Senior Counsel John Rogers for the NWHB, Sophia insisted that the evidence the Board required was available. 'They just didn't take the space to talk to me personally about the abuse in the family home.' Mr Rogers put it to Sophia that she would have been 'a very tender little person to be bringing into a courtroom' at the age of nine. 'You wouldn't bring me into a courtroom at nine years of age,' she retorted. 'You would take me into a home and a caring situation and you would talk to me and ask me what was wrong and who was beating me up and breaking my bones and who was inflicting all the damage on me. That is what you would do.'

Mr Rogers said:

The very point is that that is what people would do now. At that time, they didn't have the legal powers to do it. This is the difficulty. You see, Sophia, you were seen as a child to have been beaten, but the view of the case conference was that there was no more that could be done, in the light of your father's denial, than conduct what was described as 'voluntary supervision', which was the only course open. . . You see, the view taken, Sophia, was that there was no sound legal basis for an action by the Health Board which would take you into care, given the evidence.

The case conference to which Mr Rogers was referring took place on 11 August 1979. It was convened by Dr J. K. Heagney, the then Director of Community Care for Sligo and Leitrim the North Western Health Board, and as such the person charged with overall responsibility for managing cases of suspected non-accidental injury of children. The idea of such conferences is to bring together the key professionals involved in working with a particular client or family, to share information and devise strategies. Mr Duffy, who had worked for some years in Birmingham in England, was familiar with the procedure, then relatively new in Ireland.

Among those gathered at Markievicz House to discuss Sophia McColgan were Mr Duffy, Dr McDonagh and Ms Taheny. Dr Dunleavy was not asked to attend and nor was Dr Desmond Moran, the McColgan family's GP. Dr McDonagh wrote to Dr Moran later in the month informing him of the conclusions reached and asking him to keep in touch 'should any problems arise'.

Dr McDonagh told the conference that Sophia's injuries were consistent with her story, but that other causes could not be ruled out. McColgan had told Dr McDonagh the same story he told the social workers: the nose injury had occurred accidentally after he had pushed his daughter, and that all the family's troubles arose from having to live with his parents-in-law. Dr McDonagh recommended that Sophia should be discharged from hospital and that social workers should keep in contact with the family. Mr Duffy warned that the social worker who had been involved in the case, Ms Taheny, found McColgan very difficult to deal with, and had more influence with Mrs McColgan. He said, though, that she could maintain family contact.

The conference concluded that there was no sound legal basis for an action by the Health Board because the medical evidence would not prove non-accidental injury. It was decided that the only option was voluntary supervision and that this was to continue. Sophia was going home.

'I just could not believe it when they told me,' she said. 'To this day I cannot believe that.' McColgan had moved the family into the cottage at Cloonacurra, away from Sally and Michael, the people McColgan had described as his interfering in-laws, but who were seen by the children as their only protection. Sophia knew as she walked through the door of her father's house that summer day that she was in deep trouble. She did not have long to wait to feel the force of his rage for her act of defiance. 'He closed the door and he got a brush and he just charged at me,' she said. 'He got me into a very small space between the toilet and the wall and he rammed the brush handle repeatedly into my stomach. He used tremendous force. I was completely winded and doubled up with the pain.' The man who had persuaded the authorities that his family needed privacy left his little daughter crumpled in the bathroom, from which she would later crawl to her bed.

'I was violently sick for days,' Sophia said. 'I thought I was going to die. I really mean that. I was in so much pain that I thought I could not survive. I even wanted to die. My protest had been in vain. I thought to myself, no matter how much you tell them, they are not going to believe you. Gerry had run away so many times and he had told so many people. He was like a hare. I couldn't run because I would only slow him down and anyway he was always brought back. Now this. They didn't listen and that was a huge shock to me. I knew for certain that I would die if I ever had to go through pain as bad as that again. I had to find some other way of going on. I suppose I decided then that I would have to protect myself and avoid the flames. It seemed to me that he was being allowed to carry on his abuse of the entire family. I was silenced.'

2

'I FELT SO LOVED...'

When Joseph McColgan presented himself on the doorstep of Sally and Michael's house in Ballinacarrow for the first time in 1966, he had never heard of Patsy. He had met one of her sisters at a dance in Strandhill and had come calling to bring her out again. The sister wasn't in, and it was Patsy who went to the door. McColgan was twenty-four. Patsy was nineteen. Photographs from that period show McColgan dapper and slim in a tight suit and winklepicker shoes. Patsy said she felt sorry for him, all dressed up and nowhere to go. When he asked her would she like to come out herself, she said, 'Why not?' Within a year, they were married.

'Wasn't my sister lucky? Wasn't I misfortunate?' said Patsy with a small, bleak smile. 'I didn't know anything about him or about his family. It was crazy really, getting married to someone you don't know. He was working in England and I'd see him every few weeks. There was no sign then that he was a bully. I thought a lot of him. After we were married, we moved to London, and then to the north of England. I would say we were married a while before he first put his fists up to me.'

Sally said she was never comfortable with McColgan. 'He seemed a nice enough man, but he was a stranger to me when she told me they were getting engaged,' she said. 'I said to Patsy, "Take your time." But I didn't want to kick up a fuss.'

Patsy gave up her job as a telephonist to go with her husband to England. She didn't write home very often. The couple stayed with relations in London for a while, and Gerry was born there in 1969. Sophia was born a year later, on 17 May 1970, in a town in Yorkshire. Patsy had to call the ambulance herself because her husband would not bring her to the hospital. It was a week before he visited his first-born daughter. There was confusion about Sophia's birthday — at first it was recorded as 14 June, and later she was told it was 14 May. Her mother recently told her it was 17 May.

'The violence really started after I had the children,' said Patsy. 'It was jealousy, I think. He began to get very aggressive. It got worse as the years went on and worse the more kids I had. In England we had arguments, but because I was working day and night, I was seldom at home. We had very little time to be together having violent arguments or rows.'

Patsy had discovered quickly enough that her husband could not hold down a job. He worked for a while on the buses, but gave it up after rows with other workers. It was left to her to be the breadwinner, while he tinkered about with old boats and cars in a garage beside their estate house. Patsy worked as a bus conductor, doing double shifts all week and often also working on her days off.

Sophia has memories of those days, the start of the bad memories. 'I remember being in a big empty room. There was just a cot and I was standing up in the cot reaching up my arms. There was no one else in the room. I could hear my mother outside trying to come in, but my father was telling her not to. I don't know how he was stopping her. I just know she wanted to come to me and he wouldn't let her.' Sophia said that sometimes she was not allowed to see her mother for long periods. She remembers being in the room with Gerry. There were no toys.

Later, when she was able to walk, her father would bring her to collect Patsy from the bus station. 'I had to be perfect,' she said. 'I had all these pretty little dresses, and I would wear one of those and my hair would be combed and put up in plaits. My hair was curly and it was hard to comb it out straight. My socks had to be at exactly the right height. I remember once I had spilled something on the front of my dress and we were supposed to be going out to visit his friend. We were late. My father saw that the dress was stained and he started to shout at me. I remember I was very small and he was very big, shouting and roaring down at me. I was terrified. I was ordered to get changed immediately.'

There was cruelty with a more perverse edge too. 'One time he put my shoes on the wrong feet and made me walk like that across the town to collect my mother from work. My feet were sore and bleeding and when we got back to the house he blamed me for putting the shoes on wrong, even though I wasn't old enough even to tie my own shoelaces. He hit me. He'd cook and it would always be spaghetti, which Gerry and I didn't like. He would shout at us to eat it, and my mother would try to eat ours up for us. He used to beat Gerry even then. He brought us to a kids' pool once, and he ducked our heads under the water. Once we got headlice and we were scrubbed for days on end.'

One day McColgan came home with a doll for Sophia. 'He had bought me a walking, talking Cindy doll about three feet high. She had long hair and a lovely dress. He put her on top of the wardrobe. Now and again he'd take her down and say she was for me. She had records that you put in her back. I waited over a year,

30

looking at the box on top of the wardrobe, and then he took it down one time we were going to Ireland and he brought it and gave it to my aunt.'

McColgan was unsettled in England, and wanted to get home to Sligo. He decided that it would be better if the children were sent home first, so that, he said, he and Patsy could concentrate on making enough money to buy a farm back home. 'It was he who asked me if I'd take the children,' recalled Sally. 'And then he was casting it up all over the years that it was Patsy who had sent them to us and cut him off from them.' She sighed. 'I was used to dealing with people that if they said a thing they meant it.' Asked now how she felt all those years before about being separated from her infants, Patsy McColgan replied, 'I used to be kind of lonely and heartbroken.'

Sally was happy to take the children. She had done the same for one of her brothers for a while, and she loved the little ones. Gerry was quite sick when he came home, and she nursed him back to health. Her dislike of her son-in-law grew each time she met him. 'Once when they were here visiting, Patsy was putting up his dinner for him and he let out a shout that it was too hot,' she said. 'He used to shout at her a lot. I wasn't sure if he was beating her. I didn't want to be seen as someone who was prowling about watching.'

Sophia's voice softens as she remembers the years she and her siblings spent with their Granny and Grandad in Ballinacarrow. She laughs with delight at the childishness of the memories. She was three when she came back permanently.

Those were great times. Gerry and I were there together first and then Michelle was sent home to Granny's when she was just a few months old. She had pneumonia. We'd run in and out, and we played with friends, children who lived in the village. We picked green berries off the bushes and made lanes for races on the lawn, and then we'd fight over who won and scoff the sweets we'd got from Grandad for prizes. Gerry was always good at running. Granny and Grandad would let us have sweets, or a bag of crisps out of the shop, and Grandad would make us up a drink with lemonade and ice-cream. We played basketball too.

We played hide-and-seek in the bushes and we had Doodle. He was our dog and he was brilliant. He used to be able to roll a ball along his back and headbutt it. When he was killed on the road, we bawled our eyes out for weeks. Later on we got another dog, Bruce, and he was a great companion. We had a friend called Mary and she was about sixteen then, but she had Down's syndrome, and she'd come in and play as well. She was nice. She still comes in to Granny's. We'd paint and draw. I was friends with the schoolteacher's daughter, and one day she brought me down to the other shop and got two little go-go things for each of us to put our hair in pony tails. They were purple and pink and I thought this was absolutely brilliant. I thought it was magic because she didn't have to pay for them. I think it was that her mother was to pay for them later. My mother sent us boxes of clothes, and a doll for each of us once.

Then came schooldays. The school is just across the road from the house. At three o'clock when school finished, Granny would bring us in to do our lessons and she would help us. We watched our Great-Granny smoking and we decided to try it so we got cigarettes from the shop and I sent Gerry in to Granny for matches. We were caught anyway sitting under a tree smoking, and Granny ate us. She gave out rings and she said she'd get a stick to us. But it was just an idle threat. She explained to us that smoking was only for grown-ups and it was bad for you, and that we could have set the place on fire. I listened to her. Later on she made it up with us and gave us sweets. Other times if she was cross with us over something, we'd be put to bed early. We tried smoking rolled up pieces of newspaper one time as well.

Granny used to worry about our health and on damp evenings if we were out playing late, she'd tell us there was a man up the road who'd come and take us away in his van if we didn't come in. She used to allow us make toast at the front of the range and that was a great occupation. Then there were visitors and we would go in to see what they were like and what they might be getting to eat. Brother Norbert used to come from the monastery at Cloonamahon and had a great big sweet tooth. When he came, there was Swiss Roll, and that suited me. You'd always get the best of things when there were visitors. When Granny got a television we were allowed to watch it after we had our homework done. We watched puppet shows like 'Wanderly Wagon' and cartoons like 'Tom and Jerry'. I remember watching Shirley Temple on TV. She had curly hair like me. I loved her.

Granny used to make things. She showed me how to knit and sew and do embroidery. She was always out with her sewing machine fixing something and I used to love to help her. One Christmas time she made me a sewing box. I thought this was the bee's knees. This was the sun and the moon and the stars. Some of the girls at school got them too but they were shop bought. The one Granny made me was huge, all covered with lovely paper. She put lovely soft satin inside and loads of pockets for me. She made it for me. She also got us lots of books, cookery books and different things. Gerry liked fishing so she got him books about that.

There was a little pond beside the shop and we would catch frogs there and put them in jars to watch them swimming. Sometimes we would be allowed go down the village and one day we tried these banana penny chews and we liked them so much we bought a load of them. We would take off our socks and shoes and play with our friends in the little river. It was only a few inches deep so it was safe for us. Sometimes we'd release a frog into the river, and then we'd think he was going on a magical journey and that he'd end up in America. We used to think all these things.

Then there were the old people in the village. There was an old lady who went round in long black dresses and capes. She was a bit daft. She used to go to funerals and jump into graves. We'd say hello to her. Gerry used to call me a sissy because he could ride Granda's bike and for a long time I was too small to climb up on Granny's. After I managed to be able to climb up and pedal it, we'd get on the bikes and go for a spin out the road to see Mrs O'Connor, who had a monkey. The monkey was lovely. He was a great joke as well. He was always escaping. He had figured out how to let himself out of his cage, but Mrs O'Connor hadn't cottoned on to that. We would all be going around searching for the monkey. He got killed then one time he had let himself out. There was a big farmers' protest going through the village and he got knocked down.

All the characters used to come into Granny's shop. There was a man I thought was a magician. He said he could turn me into a crocodile and back again. I was worried, though, because he also said he had turned someone into a frog and they never changed back again. There was a bakery man who used to give me a box of iced buns, all for myself. We played hide-and-seek under the counter. There was a little hatch door just my size, and Gerry would never find me there, so I usually gave up hiding.

One man came into the shop, and he always had a woman's handbag with him, a different one each day. One day, a young German man was hitching a lift outside and Grandad asked him in for tea. He came every year after that and he brought me a jigsaw puzzle of a dog. He brought his friends, and then his wife. His name was Horst, and one year he arrived in an old gypsy caravan with two big horses, and they parked up the field. We used to run up after school and get horse rides. I remember getting soaked in the long grass and Granny giving out.

One day, I watched my auntie painting the gates and I decided to paint my doll's cradle. I found a tin of purple paint. I got all covered in the paint and Granny nearly had a fit. My aunt had a dolls' house and Great-Granny Mullen gave her nice wallpaper for each of the eight rooms. It was brilliant. We had furniture to put in it. One day, my aunt went into town on the bus and arrived back with a dressing table and a chair for the bedroom. I used to wash my dolls on the lawn and Granny gave me my very own blue, round basin to wash Dora in.

Days we'd go to the chapel with Grandad. Gerry loved that. I'd go for the craic. In May Grandad would have little rosary sessions for Our Lady. People would be having their confessions heard. You helped Grandad. You'd light a candle, and you'd bless people and wish them luck. I'd say a few prayers. It was kind of a special time. You felt important. We knew many's the people in those days and we had loads of friends, especially when we went to school. I felt so loved by both of my grandparents. Nothing was wrong and I had so much freedom.

The only hard times in those few happy years occurred when the children's parents would come home for visits, or when the children would be sent to England for holidays. McColgan had beaten Gerry with a horse crop during one such visit. 'I liked to see my mother,' said Sophia. 'I didn't really know my parents. I knew my mother loved me, because she was always hugging me when she came home and she was delighted to see me. But I remember when they were coming, I'd run into Granny's from school and ask, "Is he here? Is he here?" I didn't want him to be there. I was afraid of him. Even before he started.'

Before he 'started' in earnest, McColgan gave his children a taste of what was to come. During a summer visit in 1975, he took them, in the peculiar three-wheeled car he'd built in England, to the beach at Rosses Point, a few miles north-west of Sligo. There, unobserved by the other families enjoying the sunshine and the waves, he staged, for Gerry, Sophia and Michelle, a mock drowning. He took each of the children out into the water separately and he pushed each little head down under the waves and held it there. 'I couldn't breathe and I needed to breathe and he was holding me down,' said Sophia. 'Then at the very last moment he let me come up for air.' Back on the shore, McColgan pretended that he had been teaching the children to swim. Sally remembers that the children were strange that evening when they came back to Ballinacarrow. 'Gerry told me that his father had taken him out into the waves and tried to drown him,' she said. 'The next day, they were to go again. Gerry kicked up and was crying and screaming and saying he didn't want to go. I thought he was just being pettish and childish. Joe McColgan grabbed him and threw him into the car. Gerry had no choice. I didn't want to interfere, in case McColgan took it out on me.'

McColgan, with the money saved from Patsy's earnings in England, had bought the cottage in Cloonacurra and two acres of land for £700 in 1975. The children were told that their mother and father were coming home to stay. 'I remember saying to Gerry, "I don't want him to come here. I hate him,"' said Sophia. 'Gerry felt the same. Then I felt bad about feeling that. We were taught at school that you were supposed to love your parents and obey them and that Mums and Dads knew everything. But I was afraid.'

The parents came back at Christmas in 1976. Patsy was pregnant. The plan was that they would stay with her parents until McColgan got the cottage fixed up, and then the young family would move there. McColgan's return changed the atmosphere in the house in Ballinacarrow irrevocably. 'He was always complaining about something,' Sophia said. 'I never called him anything but Joe — but he soon changed that when he came home for good. He beat it into us to calling him Daddy,' she said.

The cottage at Cloonacurra was a dump. It was small, damp and falling down. The land around it, beside the river, was rushy and waterlogged. Sally watched with growing dismay McColgan's pathetic attempts to make it habitable. 'He'd go down there every day but he did nothing. A good man would have had it plastered. He just hadn't a clue,' she said.

McColgan would say that he was bringing the children down to the cottage with him for company. In reality, playing after school had now been replaced in the children's lives by hard labour and abuse. 'He would have us out in the fields gathering stones,' Sophia said. 'If you didn't get enough, you'd be dragged into the house and walloped. We had to help put in concrete floors. We'd make up the cement and carry it in to him in buckets. Then he was building a wall, and we had to bring him the cement and he would be putting iron bars in and he'd pour in the cement. You'd be just praying it would turn out all right, because if it didn't, somebody would get beaten or thumped or belted. Whatever kind of tool he had to hand he would use it across your body.'

Gerry was eight when his father hit him on the back of his head with a spanner. McColgan then made him put his hood up to cover the wound, and made him hitch with him into Sligo to exchange some nails. That night, the little boy collapsed on the road on his way home. His head was caked with blood and there was blood on his clothes. When Patsy asked her husband what had happened, he told her he had thrown the spanner onto a window ledge and it hit Gerry because the child was in the way. McColgan had made Gerry work until the early hours of the morning. The child had to hold a torch when it got dark. One time, in the middle of the winter, Sally ventured to say to McColgan that he shouldn't have the child up working so late especially on cold and frosty nights. 'Mind your own fucking business,' he replied.

'Patsy usen't to tell me anything,' said Sally. 'She'd have black eyes and marks on her face and I'd ask her what happened and she'd say, "A stick hit me," or something. She didn't want to upset me, and I didn't want to be seen as the kind of person who goes nosing around in other people's marriages, which is how I *would* have been seen.'

Around this time, the family got something of a reprieve, when McColgan mysteriously lost the power of his legs for several weeks. 'He was always depressed, and this particular time, whatever psychological ailment he had, it left him in a wheelchair. It was a break for Gerry and me, because he was out of action,' said Sophia.

One day, McColgan said he had had enough and he was leaving. 'Granny had said something to him about not liking the way he was treating us children. She told him he was too hard on us. He got out a suitcase and I thought, "This is great." I was euphoric,' said Sophia. 'He packed all his fancy shirts and ties. He had all these multicoloured shirts and he had dickie bows made of purple and green velvet. He had so many pairs of shoes you wouldn't believe it. Shoes with red circles and green dots, blue stripes, leopardskin, you name it. After he was put in prison in 1995, we found fifteen fertiliser bags full of the shoes he'd brought back from England with him in the Seventies.'

'He took a great interest in his appearance at that time. Everything would be shining on him. The teeth would be shining, the shoes would be shining. I suppose it was his way of saying to people, "I'm in control of my life. I look great." But he was the person at the end of the day who was totally out of control of his life. He had no control over anything. The only way he could try to make people think otherwise was by trying to impress them as a gentleman. Anyway, this day he had his tweed coat on and he was going. Nobody said a word to stop him. Nobody wanted him to stay. But it was all just a sulk. He went nowhere.'

***

Sophia was frequently expected to mind little Michelle, who was two years younger than her. Once, when Michelle was four, she came into the house covered with a skin rash. 'There was a field of buttercups outside. It was bright yellow and Michelle had been picking them. My father said I had poisoned her. He demanded to know what I had given her. "Dozie Sophie, what did you give Michelle?" he said. She was going to die, according to him, and it was my fault. I got a terrible beating. He kept thumping my ears and then he rushed her off to Dr Moran. He and my mother and Michelle hitched into Sligo. Later on, they came back in Granda McColgan's Volkswagen Beetle with Granny and Granda McColgan and there wasn't a word about it. It turned out it was just an allergic reaction and Michelle was fine. But he had me convinced I had killed my little sister.'

Schoolwork was scrutinised for excuses to punish. McColgan battered Sophia for drawing a picture on the blank top part of a page in a copy book which was designed for writing and drawing. 'I had written whatever I was meant to write, like, "It is Tuesday, the sun is shining," and I'd drawn a house with the sky above it and the sun,' she said. 'He beat me for wasting paper with drawing.'

After the first time her father raped her, at Derreen Bog, near Ballymote in County Sligo, when she was six, Sophia said she went into a state of shock and terror. Her Granny had organised for a neighbour, Mrs McGuinn, who was the village dressmaker, to make the little girl's First Communion dress. 'I thought I was beautiful in it, but I was very unhappy,' said Sophia. 'The rapes continued, in the field, the shed, the loft. The second time was in the shed at Cloonacurra. I remember the agonising pain and afterwards going off to play with my dolls to try and forget. There were so many incidents I thought he'd never stop. I was petrified with fear. I was bewildered and horrified, but I also thought maybe this was normal, this was what fathers did to their daughters. I knew I was supposed to obey him, but I didn't want him near me. I didn't want to be a bad girl, and I thought I'd be a bad girl if I didn't love my father, even though I hated him. I was so hurt. I was like someone whose leg has been cut off there and then, and

I was there holding the leg that had been cut off and it was still hurting. It was so, so horrific to me that I just couldn't open my mouth.'

'On the actual day of my First Communion, my grandfather put flowers in the chapel and on the hedge outside Granny's. Grandad made badges with the Sacred Heart on them and medals for all the children in the Communion class. That was lovely. My father made me walk to the church with my head held very high. He did not like the way I walked and he was always beating me over it. He used to compare me to people who had a disability and couldn't walk properly. There was a man in the village who was handicapped in some way. His feet turned in very badly and his body was all to one side. My father said I walked like him. He would make fun of me. He was always standing on my feet and grinding his boots into them. I still have terrible problems with my feet to this day.'

Sophia walked, stilted and sore all over, full of pain, down through the village in her white Communion shoes. Her misery is evident in the photographs she has kept of the occasion. The then chaplain at Ballinacarrow gave her that First Communion. He is elderly now and has retired. He declined to be interviewed for this book. 'I wouldn't want to be involved in a situation like that,' he said. 'I knew the father, of course, but I would never have been talking to any of them about family matters.'

McColgan had started to cut the children off from other people. Sophia asked a little girlfriend down to the cottage one day while McColgan was burning weeds off a field. 'I got her to ask him could she stay, and, to keep up appearances, he said she could. She and I sat and watched the blaze and we thought it was great, like a bonfire,' Sophia said. 'But after she went home, he beat me and forbade me to play with other children again.'

The fact that the family was sleeping at her grandparents' house in Ballinacarrow, was, Sophia feels, some sort of restraining influence on McColgan, but he was agitating for a move to the cottage. The children dreaded this development. 'I remember begging Granny to let us children stay with her,' said Sophia. 'She said, "Sophia, I love you very much and I will always be here for you. But I can't keep you. He would get the Gardaí to come and bring you back to him. We can't keep you, legally. He is your father."'

McColgan deeply resented the affectionate relationship the children had with their maternal grandparents, and, more importantly, he was unable to have total control in a household of which he was not the head, and in which other adults had some authority. His father-in-law used to tell him to stop if he caught him hitting the children. When Sally brought Sophia to Sligo General Hospital in July 1979, it was the ultimate outrage as far as he was concerned. She had interfered once too often. During a visit to Sophia in hospital, McColgan told social worker Deirdre Taheny that what was needed was for them to 'break links with their own parents and establish themselves as an independent family'. And so it was that McColgan moved his wife and children out of Ballinacarrow and into the cottage at Cloonacurra. Gerry was ten, Sophia nine, Michelle seven and Keith three. Patsy was pregnant.

Sophia was discharged from hospital towards the end of August 1979. Ms Taheny was the social worker assigned to visit the family. She recorded that all seemed to be well, though at one point she noted that the children seemed subdued. She attempted to persuade McColgan that it was important to maintain contacts with the outside world, but he shouted her down, raving about interfering neighbours and the need to make a complete break with his in-laws. Ms Taheny observed that McColgan made no effort in her company to exercise any control over three-year-old Keith, who was being cheeky and using bad language. She noted that McColgan informed her, 'It is necessary to give children a free rein to develop themselves.'

In truth, McColgan had already initiated little Keith into his world of violence. When Keith was a baby, his father had pressed his tiny hand down onto the roasting hot top of the kitchen range, holding it there while the baby screamed. Keith still has the scars. Ms Taheny walked with Patsy to collect the children from school and reported that Mrs McColgan told her that all was well.

A month later, on 24 October 1979, Gerry was admitted to Sligo General Hospital with strangle marks on his neck and bruises all over his body. Dr Doreen Dunleavy had once again been called out, this time by Michael. Gerry had been thrashed with a metal strap and seized by the neck. Dr Dunleavy wrote another letter of referral to casualty staff:

> Please see again another child of the McColgan family. Case of child battering. Sophia, another child was hospitalised a month ago [*sic*] with the same problem. Dr Heagney's office [i.e. the social work department] was notified and social worker has made contact.
>
> This child is a nervous wreck . . . Father grabbed child by neck two nights ago, over some trivial matter. Marks on neck noted. Father has an uncontrollable temper. Please advise . . .

3

STOLEN
CHILDHOOD

'Come away, O human child!
To the waters and the wild
With a faery, hand in hand,
For the world's more full of weeping than you can understand.'
(from 'The Stolen Child' by W. B. Yeats)

'My childhood was stolen from me,' said Sophia. Apart from death, there is nothing worse than what we went through. Really, my father's house was like a military camp. We were not allowed to talk to anyone. People we loved, we were no longer allowed to see. He would collect us from school and we would be marched down the village in single file. When he got us into the house, the interrogations would begin. He would line us up as if we were about to be shot, and he would walk up and down shouting at us. 'Who were you talking to today? I told you not to speak to anyone. Didn't I? What did I tell you?' You had to answer, and if you gave the wrong answer, you would get beaten.

If you thought you had the right answer and you said, 'I'll never talk to anyone again,' he would say, 'That's not what I told you.' He'd change it, twist it around so that he could beat you more. He'd say, 'What did I tell you? You are not allowed to talk to anyone at school and you are not allowed to talk to anyone without telling me first.' Or he might beat you because your hair was tossed, or one of the younger ones had tossed hair and you were supposed to have tidied it, or some such reason.

My father was very good at trying to turn one child against another. He'd ask Michelle, say, 'What did Sophia do today?' And she'd be punished if she didn't come up with something. Michelle might then say something against me to take the heat off her, and I'd hate her for telling a lie on me. It might be something like, 'She was at the wall of the school and she was talking to Granny.' She would then have been praised as the good child who told. He'd roar at me, 'Why did you do it? Why did you do it?' Then he would beat me. He beat your hands, your legs, your body. He would get one child to go across the road and cut a sally rod to beat one of the other children. After he had beaten me, he'd send Gerry out for another rod and if the rod Gerry brought back wasn't the right sort, he'd beat Gerry with it, and then he'd send someone else out for more. If you brought a good rod, you'd be praised for it. He had cut us off from all our friends; now he was isolating us from each other. It was a way of emotionally turning us against each other. He worked hard at that.

In this way, the children became afraid to speak, even to each other, even if their father was out of the house. There was always the risk that someone would break under interrogation and denounce one of the other children. There would be complete silence in the house, and then, after an outbreak of extreme violence, it would be filled with screams and sobbing. Gerry's hair all fell out and Dr Moran treated him for alopecia.

Sophia does remember one conversation she and Gerry had about rods. 'We were trying to decide which type hurt the least. We agreed that a thick rod hurt less than a thin one, and a thick one might break, but the thin ones were flexible and never broke. With them, he was able to get up a greater speed raising the rod high up over our heads and lashing down on us. Sometimes he used blackthorn sticks and then the thorns would be stuck in your hands for days.'

'Gerry was a very brave boy,' Sophia acknowledges. 'He often took the rap for me. He took beatings for me, by owning up to something after my father had set me up for it. I covered for Gerry too. He'd run away, and hours later my father would demand to know where he was, and I'd say that he had just that minute run away. We used to be locked in a room together. We were cold and hungry and we couldn't get to the toilet. In the end, we had to go on the floor. Gerry managed to escape out the window and he ran to neighbours. He was always running away, and my father would be out on the tractor driving around searching for him and telling everybody what a brat he was. It was like a hunt. A blood sport, like hounds after a poor defenceless animal. My father would alert the Gardaí and then they would have to join in the search.

'Gerry ran to Ballymote, to Ballina, even, once, to Dublin. Imagine the intelligence that took, for a child to get away, catch trains, find addresses, make his way to people. He told everybody about the beatings. The Gardaí would bring him home. Neighbours would bring him home. Relations would bring him home. But he kept on trying.' Sally also remembers the Gardaí bringing Gerry home. 'They told him he was under sixteen, he'd have to go home to his father,' she said.

Sophia's voice still shakes when she speaks about an incident in which Gerry was made to strip before being thrashed with a carpet beater. 'We were all terrified. He was screaming and begging for mercy. We thought he was going to be killed. Even my mother thought he was going to die, it was so severe. I remember once my mother was screaming and crying at my father to stop beating one of us children and he turned around and nearly knocked her out with a punch. The beatings and interrogations could go on until the early hours of the morning. Or until someone bled, or got sick or peed on the floor. A sort of calmness came over him then, as if he had achieved something. You tried not to cry, because that made him worse. He hated you to show emotion. You'd be so sore you wouldn't be able to stand up or sit down.'

Patsy McColgan remembers the family having to sit 'like a court' while someone was being questioned. 'It was like a cult,' she said. 'It was brainwashing.' In the High Court damages hearing, Counsel for the NWHB claimed that there was contributory negligence on the part of Patsy McColgan, because she knew what was happening to her children, and did nothing to stop it.

Patsy knows, looking back, that there was much she did not grasp about what was going on in her home. 'I thought things would improve after I went back to the old fella,' she said. (She often calls her former husband 'the old fella' or Joe McColgan or 'the old buck'.) 'Then when the social workers were coming after Sophia came out of hospital, he used to spend a lot of time with his parents in Sligo, and that helped. I don't know what he was doing — he could have been up to anything for all I know. It seemed to me there were periods when things quietened down.

Things were better when the social workers were calling. But maybe it wasn't like that for the kids. I suppose my mind has blanked out a lot of what happened.' I would have always been working too. I did most of the work, looking after the animals and running the place. The house really wasn't fit to live in. Maybe I didn't notice the half of what was going on.'

There was no washing machine or other modern equipment in the cottage, and there were babies whose terry towelling nappies had to be washed along with all the rest of the family's clothes. Sophia remembers that her mother's hands were always ruined with dermatitis. 'They were like a man's hands, all red and rough and chapped.'

'He was very cunning too,' said Patsy. 'It was said in the High Court that he was of low intelligence. I think that was a very wrong assumption. He had everybody sussed out into a square box. He had everybody's movements monitored, and then he was watching to see if anything went wrong with his plans and could he do anything about it. You'd get him out the door and he'd say he was going off somewhere and you'd be relieved. Next thing, a minute later, he'd be back. He was watching everyone. He could nearly tell what you were thinking.' Sophia remembers that her father wore black leather gloves, and he had the habit of deliberately leaving one of them behind him, so that he could return into a company he had just left, and find out if people were talking about him. 'He'd listen at doors too, including official doors.'

There was also the violence that McColgan inflicted on his wife. 'He beat her to a pulp,' said Sophia. 'He broke her. She was a broken person.' The children had to watch while their father beat their mother until her clothes were torn and she was bleeding and pleading for mercy. They watched as he made her strip off her clothes and then he threw a bucket of cold water over her. They watched him kick her in the stomach and the groin while she was pregnant. 'My mother was really an object. She had to jump and dance attendance on him at all times. She had to put his shoes and socks on him every day. He gave her orders and she had to obey. Otherwise, she would get a punch in the face or her hair pulled out or whatever. She had not even any privacy. There were no boundaries in that house. She could not help us. She was one of us.'

Senior Counsel Patrick Hanratty, representing Dr Moran in the High Court, put it to Sophia that it was 'astonishing' that her mother did not tell her doctor that she was being physically abused. 'She was terrorised,' said Sophia. 'She was a victim. She had to say exactly what he said. She had to agree with him and if she didn't, she got violent abuse. It is not astonishing.'

Patsy McColgan, remembering her marriage, put it simply. 'His word was law. I had no one to talk to. Friends were out. Friends cost you money, he'd say. In England people keep to themselves. After we were back in Ireland, it wasn't always the same. There might be a quiet enough time when the extreme violence would stop and then he would just go berserk. Any excuse he found, he'd go completely insane. He'd keep you up till two or three in the morning ranting and raving. I was too soft. You lose so much self-confidence, and if you're married you've even less footing to stand your ground. He always managed it that he was running the show. In the morning you had to get up and work. He'd sit in a chair and say he wasn't feeling well.'

Conditions in the cottage were appalling. There was no electricity and very little furniture. The extension McColgan had designed was faulty and unfinished. Walls were not plastered. There were no curtains, just pieces of cloth which would be pinned up. It was cold and damp. The children were not fed in a regular way. 'Sometimes there was food, but it would be very poor,' said Sophia. 'He would go into Sligo and come home with a load of something he'd seen cheap. Like fifty packets of Club Goldgrain, it was one time. Or a big heap of loaves of stale bread that had been reduced. Or tins of beans. One time there was nothing to eat in the house except apples. He made us eat this margarine which was gone off. It was disgusting. We hated it. He'd buy horrible meat sometimes and make it into a hot curry which was totally unsuitable for children. My father would not let my mother feed us; she had to feed him. She was not allowed to give us any attention. That was another way he isolated her from us.'

In the middle of all the violence, McColgan had notions for his children. 'He used to make us go to music classes at the Ursuline Convent in Sligo,' said Sophia.

He bought Gerry and me two violins. He arranged a lift for us in a meat van to his parents' house on the Circular Road, and then they'd take us to the Ursuline. It was the late Sister Kevin who taught us. Gerry was quite good. I was hopeless. All I could manage was 'The Bells of the Angelus'. My father would get very frustrated. He had bought me this fancy violin and I couldn't play it.

Then, for some uncanny reason, he bought me this concert flute. It cost a lot of money. He was always talking about James Galway and he insisted I learn it. He got a man in to teach me. I didn't like him. When neighbours came, or relations, my father would make us play for them. I remember I had to play for an aunt and some cousins. The pads under the keys were all worn out and cracked and I made a lot of mistakes. I remember going bright red as he gave out to me. I was dreading the beating I'd get when they left.

He had this ritual at night. Gerry and I had to play for him and when one of us would make a mistake, you'd be walloped and sent into the back room. 'Go and practise,' he'd roar. Then you'd be brought back and the routine would be repeated. This went on like a mad thing he had in his head for four or five hours. In my mind, I'd be pleading, 'Please let this end.' I didn't say it because he would only have made you go on longer. Tears made him worse. Pain was the stimulus he loved. He was very cruel.

One of the girls who went to national school with Sophia remembers her as a shy, quiet child. 'In a way, she seemed normal, but there was always an element of fear in her. She liked to be away from home. Her father used to come to school at lunchtime and stay with her and her brother and sister in the schoolyard. For a while, we thought they were lucky to have a Daddy who did that. Looking back, I suppose he was stopping them from mixing with the rest of us.'

McColgan was, the schoolfriend said, a very respected man in the community. 'He was always dressed to the nines, and very mannerly. He would insist on carrying my mother's shopping out to the car, and he'd hold open the door for you. But I was always wary of him. I saw him as a weirdo. We knew he was physically violent. We knew he'd broken Sophia's nose and run over Gerry's legs with the tractor. You'd see Patsy out at all hours doing very hard, physical work. He seemed to rule his family with an iron fist. He used to bring them to chapel in relays, and they used to have to wait in line outside and then he would order them to march in behind him to the front row. We children held all these things against him. But he was very respectable.'

A young man from the village said that when McColgan marched his family to the front of the church, it was always ten minutes after mass had started. 'He made this big entrance, the great family man, and his children had to walk in behind him like ducks. I always had a bad feeling about him because I had heard stories. One time, I heard, Patsy ran away from him and he followed her with a knife. Once I was doing work at my house and he came to me wanting to do some digging with an old JCB he had got, but I didn't want him about the place. Another time, I had occasion to be down at the house at Cloonacurra. I was shocked at the poverty of it. There was nothing in the main room only a range, a concrete floor and an old car seat. And this was a man who would spend a fortune on machinery and stuff. The children were never free to roam, but there were no obvious signs that he was violent.'

One Sunday, a visiting missioner priest preached in Ballinacarrow about violence in the home. 'He finished it up by saying that if anyone among us was suffering from that kind of abuse, they should hang on in there,' said one member of the congregation. "Persevere, persevere," he said. I thought it was scandalous. He should have been telling them to get help and get out.' McColgan, however, took a different view. He believed that the priest was directing the sermon at him, and he was furious. When he got the children back to the house, he interrogated them and drove it home to them once again that he was in charge, he would do as he pleased and he would be obeyed.

By this time, he had already established the practice of leaving mass early with Sophia. 'He would bring me back to the cottage on the tractor and he would rape me,' said Sophia. 'It took Mammy a while to get home, because she would have the messages Granny would give her, and she would have the little ones with her to manage. By the time she got home, he would have me raped.'

By the time Gerry was brought to hospital in October 1979, McColgan had completely cut his family off from the outside world. They were not allowed to go to school, or to the village, or to see Sally and Michael. Deirdre Taheny put it to the McColgans that she was concerned about the children. She noted that it was Patsy who said that Gerry had been 'quite difficult', and that McColgan had agreed. Then McColgan broke into a tirade against neighbours, relations, social workers, doctors — claiming that they were usurping his right to act as a father figure in his own home. He became aggressive and abusive towards Ms Taheny, claiming she had no right to be investigating what went on in his family. Patsy was upset and tried to intervene. He shouted at her to stop interrupting, and told Ms Taheny that he intended to bring the matter to the law 'and get to the bottom of the state interfering in their rights as parents'.

Once again, McColgan explained away Gerry's injuries as an accident which had occurred while he was giving him 'a talking to'. Ms Taheny noted that McColgan 'overreacts' to the children's misdemeanours, and could not see that children need affection and support. McColgan complained to the social worker that his mother-in-law had put her arms around Gerry, behaviour he described as 'physically over-demonstrative'.

The whole family attended a meeting at Sligo General Hospital on 31 October 1979, after the paediatrician, Dr McDonagh, referred Gerry for an intellectual assessment by psychologist Maura Armstrong. Joseph McColgan caused a scene at reception, shouting that he wanted 'no more crap' and that he was fed up with 'do-gooders interfering with his family affairs', according to Ms Armstrong's report. She found that whenever she directed a question at Patsy, it was McColgan who answered. After she pointed this out, he began to allow Patsy to speak, but when she began to say anything pertinent, he broke in with irrelevant details 'explaining that his wife was unable to recount the full history because of her quiet nature'. Ms Armstrong described his attitude to his parents-in-law as 'paranoid', while he declared that his own parents were 'a constant inspiration'. (Sophia laughed aloud and shook her head in court in 1998 when this description of her father's parents was read out.)

Gerry was still in hospital when a case conference was held on 2 November 1979. Public Health Nurse Bridie Lee had already reported concerns about McColgan's behaviour. She had learned about a showdown in the house after Patsy had walked to Cloonacurra in the company of her father. Nurse Lee told the conference that she felt the maternal grandparents were being unfairly blamed for problems in the family, adding that they had actually 'done their utmost to help'. Psychiatrist Dr Geraghty gave his assessment of McColgan as a narrow-minded, obsessional type of man, lacking insight into how children think. Dr Moran, according to Denis Duffy's note of the case conference, was 'regarded as a friend of the family'. (However, Dr Moran stated after the High Court case ended in January 1998, that while he had known of the McColgan family, the first time he had met Joseph was in his surgery in 1975. After the High Court case, he told *The Sunday Tribune* that he had a 'purely doctor/patient' relationship with McColgan.)[1] Mr Duffy noted that Dr Moran said that he had already warned McColgan of 'the consequences of his behaviour' towards the children, and felt that he had some influence with him. Ms Taheny told the conference that, because of McColgan's attitude, social work visits were 'not a useful exercise'.

It was agreed that Dr Moran would give guidance to McColgan, while Nurse Lee would 'keep an eye on the child welfare aspect of things'. Social workers would be available if their assistance was acceptable 'to the family' — but their visits to the house at Cloonacurra would cease. It was decided that it would be unwise to introduce court proceedings, since the injuries sustained by Gerry were 'not severe enough' to bring about a conviction. On 5 November 1979, Gerry was sent back to his father's house.

McColgan's control over his family was so powerful that it did not cease when he was out of the house. Nurse Lee called a few days after Gerry had come home, and noted that Patsy was influenced by her husband, to the detriment of the children. She saw Gerry arrive with a small present for his mother. Patsy put it aside, showing neither emotion nor gratitude.

The NWHB tried to arrange for the family to see a child psychiatrist from the Mater Hospital in Dublin. McColgan refused, in terms which showed that he regarded Gerry as the problem in the family rather than himself. He said he was bringing the child with him once a week to see Dr Moran and that there were 'no more problems with the boy'. On 21 December 1979, Ms Taheny recorded that the situation in the family appeared to have stabilised. 'I occasionally meet the family on the road to Ballinacarrow, but have no social contact work.'

In January 1980, Dr McDonagh wrote to Dr Moran that he had seen the McColgans at a paediatric clinic and had the impression that, despite turning down an appointment with a child psychiatrist for Gerry, 'the father is making an effort' and it was 'best to leave things as they are'. However, he stressed that a watching brief was essential. Dr McDonagh added: 'If this man gets sufficient confidence back and if the in-laws can be kept out of the situation, things might improve.'

1. Martin Wall, *The Sunday Tribune*, 25 January 1998, p. 3.

4

'DALLAS'

***

Life went on. 'I lived my life in fear,' said Sophia. 'Each day was so hard to get through back then. It was a harsh cut in my life when we went to live with my father. Then, after I was sent home from hospital that time, I really did not know how to deal with it. I hoped and prayed and I cried.'

And worked. 'He had goats and they would be tethered along the roadside. We had to gather ivy for them on our way from school. In winter, our hands would be frozen and cut from pulling at the ivy. The goats would sometimes get strangled by their tether and then we would be terrified. Who was going to tell him and take the beating? Sometimes we would be left out in the rain. Gerry had to cut wood with an axe and I had to carry the blocks across a huge dyke to the house. We would be frozen. One time we were locked out, and we were so cold we just stood there, all of us children. We had no warm coats. There was nothing to do only stand there. My mother had run away. She said she would get help. What was a little child going to do? She ran away a few times, but he would always find her and bring her back.' Patsy revealed to me that she had been given a warning after she had returned to her husband following the crisis over Sophia's hospitalisation. 'He told me then that if I ever tried to get away from him again, he would find me, no matter where I was, and he would kill me with a knife.'

'In summer, we had to gather the hay from along the roads after the council had cut the verges,' said Sophia. 'We had to rake hay in the fields. It would be hot and we would be working and there was no food or drink for us. We would be dehydrated, ready to collapse. We wouldn't stop to rest. One day my father threw a pitchfork at me and grazed my leg. My mother never had any money, but I remember one day she managed to get us a bottle of one of those cheap lemonades with saccharine in it.'

There were trips to the seaside too, but there was nothing happy or carefree about them. 'He had got us bicycles and he made us cycle ten miles over the mountains to the Salt Strands, and there he would try to drown us and then pull us out. Then we had to cycle home, and you'd be dreading what might happen when you got there.'

'My father was absolutely useless at everything. He'd spend all his money on junk. He'd buy barrels of stuff and he wouldn't even know what was in them, in case it turned out to be useful, which usually it didn't,' Sophia said. One or more of the children would have to accompany McColgan on his old tractor to collect things. He would load the trailer dangerously, and if anything fell off, a child would be beaten. On one such occasion, he ran over Gerry with the tractor, then placed Keith across his legs in the trailer to conceal a serious cut from anyone they might meet. 'Gerry was sick and in agony for days after that,' said Sophia. 'My father refused to take him to hospital until it had healed to a scab. Gerry was ordered to say it was an accident, of course.'

There was an old neighbour, Willie John, whose house adjoined the McColgan's cottage. 'He used to shout a lot, and he'd shout for someone to come and bring his water from the well,' said Sophia. 'He had a big old hearth in his kitchen and he'd sit there smoking a pipe. He had a television and we didn't, so sometimes we would go in and watch "Dallas". He'd spit these big, dirty black gobs of stuff into the fire.' At the time, Dallas-style bungalows were all the rage in Ireland, and there are plenty of them around Sligo. But to the McColgan children, the big-shouldered glitziness of filthy rich Southfork in the US soap was of another world.

Joseph McColgan was no farmer. 'He'd get doomed with animals that were sick, or too old. Then we had to look after them,' said Sophia. 'My mother and I used to be out pushing a tube down a calf's neck that he had put out too soon to grass and it had all blown up with gas and would have died. My mother had to milk the goat and I'd have to hold its legs so it wouldn't kick, and if it kicked you'd get a beating as well. He would do nothing,' she said. McColgan would often lie in bed till the middle of the day while the rest of the family slaved.

As well as the rotten house at Cloonacurra, McColgan had bought a seventy-acre mountain farm ten miles away from Cloonacurra, at Killerry. 'He'd put cows on the mountain,' said Sophia.

It was far too harsh for them there. Once he had a beautiful little Friesian cow — she was a dote — and he put her up there. She fell off a cliff and we had to get a load of people to help pull her up. She was very badly injured, but instead of having her put down, which would have been the kind thing to do, he put her in an old roofless shed on the mountain until she died.

I don't know if it's fair to say it, but he seemed to have a thing about suffering. He was cruel to animals and he'd do weird things. Like he got a vet to operate on a goat and it was as if he just wanted to see it. He took photographs of dead and injured animals. He was like a forensic scientist. And yet, when an animal died, he seemed to feel a loss from it.

A neighbour remembered a typical example of the futility of McColgan's efforts as a farmer. A cow had got loose and was drowning in a bog-hole. Neighbours helped McColgan drag the animal out and told him to warm her up or she would die. McColgan left her lying on the mountain, where she perished.

Sophia said:

There were other strange things. He would try to frighten me into thinking there were other people out there trying to get me. He'd leave you alone up the mountain and then he'd come back and say that there was someone prowling around who had been about to rape you. Your imagination would be heightened. He'd make you feel you weren't safe. It was a perversion — he'd make me feel I couldn't trust people. That they were out to get me. He told me it was a pity I was born good-looking. He'd say I was certain to be raped, and it would have been better for me to be ugly. He was weird. He almost appeared worried, and yet all this time, he was raping me.

When Sophia was six, her father had shown her a vibrator. She did not know what it was. 'I thought it was a toy,' she said. Later, he started to show her pornographic magazines. One day, when she was about eleven, and Gerry twelve, McColgan brought both of them into the loft of the cottage. 'He said he was showing us the facts of life,' said Sophia. 'He said that this had nothing to do with our mother. He tried to get us to have sex with each other. We had to take all our clothes off. He did not succeed and that made him very angry.'

Sophia's way of dealing with her father since the beating after her hospitalisation was to try to avoid challenging him. It took so little to provoke his rage and violence that her strategy had little enough effect, but it was all she could do. 'He'd say something and I would let him think I agreed. Privately, what was going through my mind was, "That's what you think. I think differently, but I'm kind of stuck." If I could get away with it, I'd say nothing. If he insisted on a reply, I'd say, "Yes." If we were out he'd turn to my mother and say, "Isn't that right, now?" She'd say, "Yes". She had to. One of his famous expressions was, "Wait till I get you home."'

Over the years, there was sometimes limited access to Sally and Michael. On Sundays, after mass, the family would be allowed to visit them. 'Granny gave us tea and sandwiches and cakes. It was a great feed for us. It was like a party,' said Sophia. 'Being fed was wonderful sometimes.' Sally would also give her daughter groceries from the shop, which Patsy would pay for with her children's allowance. She baked and sent down gingerbread and soda bread. One day she gave the children a pheasant to take home for dinner. But she had to be careful — too much help would constitute interference and would not be tolerated. The visits would be stopped and there would be violence. Sally remembers those visits and the mixed feelings she would have. 'I loved to see them, but they were afraid to talk. They weren't allowed to talk to me. He'd always be there, sitting like a guard beside them.'

'I said to Michelle once, "What happened to your hands?" They were all cut and destroyed. She said nothing. It was only years later, when all this burst open, that she told me she had had to carry cement blocks up the mountain. He listened to everything they said, and they knew what they'd get when they went home. I did my best to do all I could. I wanted to do things so that there would be no hassle, nothing to give him an excuse. He'd say, the other fellow, that I was the cause of all the trouble,' said Sally. 'I used to say nothing. I thought I'd go mad, but if I gave out I knew I'd never see them again.' Sometimes, when the children were not allowed to see her, Sally would cross the road during lunchbreak at the national school and give them sweets across the wall. This was risky — if McColgan got to hear of it, during interrogations or otherwise, there would be hell to pay. 'We would be ostracised from Granny for weeks on end,' said Sophia, 'and beaten, of course.'

The children used to be brought to Dr Moran's surgery in Stephen Street, Sligo. Sophia remembers they would be left in the old-fashioned waiting room while their father was in with the doctor. They would pass the time jumping between the hollows of the seats. 'We were sickly children,' she said. 'I never thrived. I was always covered with cuts and bruises, and I was totally withdrawn.' However, Dr Moran said he had never treated the children for any injury, nor had seen any sign of injury on them.

McColgan also brought the children to the dentist. 'That was another tragedy,' said Sophia. 'He would make me go and on the way he would be telling me all these stories about what the dentist would do to me with his big needle. He said I would get a big injection and that would be the end of me. He used to have me in an awful state. When the dentist came towards me, they would have to hold me down. I bit the dentist really hard on the finger once, I was so terrified.'

Once, when Keith was about four, Sophia was playing with him in a heap of sand beside the house.

We were on our hunkers making shapes in the sand. Keith wanted to go down to the field where my father was doing something with the tractor. I knew if he did, I would get beaten. I remember begging Keith not to do it, and not to cry. One time a couple of years before that, Keith had lost his shoe and he was crying and I got beaten.

The atmosphere in the house used to be terrible. You'd always be trying to sniff out what sort of a mood he was in. My mother used to say sometimes, 'He's like a bear today.' When he was working at something, like repairing a bit of a car, we had to sit in total silence. You daren't breathe. This might go on till two or three in the morning, with us all sitting there like robots.

In my child's mind, I thought one time that if he wasn't working, the violence might stop. I got Keith to hide my father's tools under a piece of old galvanised iron that lay at the side of the house. How wrong I was. He got angrier and angrier and said he was going to get the Gardaí. I had to try to get him to find the tools without knowing I had hidden them. In the end, I said I'd seen Keith put them there, and then all was rosy again.

In 1980, Keith was admitted to hospital with convulsions. In 1981, he was admitted to hospital twice in a two-month period, once with a lacerated eye and once with an injured finger. The following month McColgan broke Gerry's arm with a blow from a shovel. After leaving the eleven-year-old child in agony for a few days, he brought him to hospital, telling the child that if he told what had really happened, he would break the other arm for him as well. Gerry told the doctors and nurses that he'd had an accident. This appears to have been accepted without reference to his history of referral in 1979 as a 'battered child' and without reference to Keith's recent injuries. The current programme manager with the NWHB, Michael McGinley, told me that there was nothing in the 1977 departmental guidelines to indicate which personnel should be circularised with information about suspected non-accidental injuries in the past, so that the hospital staff who saw Gerry would have had no reason to query his explanation for the broken arm. Gerry was treated and sent home with his father.

And that might well have been the end of that, except that Gerry had not given up running. A few weeks later, he ran to the home of his two great-aunts in Collooney. They asked what had happened to his arm, and he told them the truth.

Nora and Peggy Lee were formidable old women, spinster sisters of Patsy's grandmother, Mrs Mullen. 'I get my strength from my great-grandmother,' said Sophia. 'She was a great believer in women's rights. She and her sisters were in Cumann na mBan, and they had done a lot when they were younger during the Troubles. Great-Granny Mullen thought we should have freedom of choice about all kinds of things. She put a few pounds in an Irish Permanent Building Society account for me. She always said a woman should keep something for her own independence.'

There was little opportunity and no encouragement for Sophia to take an interest in events in the outside world. However, she remembers the Hunger Strike posters outside the chapel in 1981, when she was ten, because of her great-grandmother's history. The posters said, 'Don't let them die.' 'I was aware that Bobby Sands was fighting for a United Ireland. We had been raised to believe that Michael Collins had been tricked into signing the Treaty, or drugged even. My father used to say he supported Bobby Sands, but then he had his own little military regime going in our house, so why would he care about the North of Ireland? There was no freedom in our house. We were prisoners too.'

The Misses Lee acted immediately when they heard Gerry's story. They called in Sergeant Tom O'Brien. O'Brien knew something of McColgan's history. Now retired and living just outside Collooney, he remembers the first time he met McColgan: 'It was shortly after he had returned to Ireland, in 1977, I think. His was the last house in my sub-district. I stopped him over an irregularity to do with his car, a three-wheel affair. The torrent of verbal abuse I got was unbelievable. I was the Gestapo, the worst of British rule, and the Lord knows what else. Later on that day, I learned that he had gone into a Garda station and made a formal two-page complaint against me. He never signed it. A while later I was helping out at the Community Games. Myself and a nun were in charge of a particular race. McColgan dragged, and I mean dragged, Gerry to the starting line, but it was the wrong race. The child was too young or too old for it. I pointed this out, and again the language out of him was ferocious. The boy was going to run because he said he was going to run. McColgan was going to have me demoted and the nun defrocked for daring to suggest otherwise.'

Sergeant O'Brien was also aware of the history of the children being hospitalised by their father. In 1979, he had phoned the social work department of the Health Board to warn that in his view McColgan was a dangerous man, and one who would threaten the law to impose his rights. Sergeant O'Brien told me that because he felt McColgan would claim he had it in for him if he was seen to be involved, he did not himself take part in the 1981 investigation of Gerry's broken arm. However, he did inform the community care department of the allegation.

Gerry made a brief statement in the presence of social worker Cathy Hynes. At Markievicz House, the file on the McColgans, which had lain dormant since 1979, was re-opened. Mr Duffy was on leave, and Maureen McManus, the formidable founder of the social work department, who had retired, was covering for him. She advised the Director of Community Care, Dr Heagney, that Joseph McColgan had stated in 1979 that social workers were not to call at his house again, and that he had been very abusive towards Ms Taheny. On his return, Mr Duffy reported to Dr Heagney that in his view, 'our previous investigations in 1979 were not evidential material in this instance as no charges arose from them and they were not the subject of this present allegation'. It was agreed that the Board would provide information about its previous involvement if a prosecution followed. There was no case conference. No letter was sent to Gerry's GP. The Gardaí meanwhile sent a file to the Director of Public Prosecutions.

On 24 April 1982, Joseph McColgan came before District Justice Alfred McMorrow at Collooney District Court, charged with assault occasioning actual bodily harm and assault to Gerry McColgan. Sophia told the High Court that Gerry was 'under house arrest' and his father did not allow him to go to court. According to Denis Duffy, social workers were not required to attend, and information about the history of non-accidental injuries and social work involvement with the family does not appear to have been put before the court. The case was adjourned for six months, and, on 20 October 1982, it was struck out. If there were any records of the court proceedings beyond the most basic facts of them having taken place, they are missing. In any case, McColgan was free to take up once again his reign of terror. He did so.

5

'YOU ARE
ALL MINE'

On a summer's day in 1983, Sophia stood with her face pressed against the window of the front bedroom at Cloonacurra. She was watching a scene outside which would dramatically change her life, and tears were streaming down her face. A woman was at the gate along with a Garda, and Joe McColgan, armed with a shovel, was shouting and roaring at them to get off his property and keep their noses out of his family's affairs. Patsy stood beside her husband, silent mostly, occasionally appearing to agree with him, occasionally taking the brunt of his rage. Above the rattle of the cement-mixer her father had left running outside the house, Sophia could hear McColgan ranting on about how everyone but himself was to blame for the problems he was having with his oldest son. He kept the tirade up for almost two hours. Sophia, who knew that Gerry had fled the house that morning, gathered that her brother was not coming home, that the woman at the gate was taking him away somewhere.

She remembers it as a day of powerfully mixed emotions. 'I was heartbroken,' she said. 'Gerry and I were so close. We loved each other so much. We were like twins. He was such a brave,

brave boy and he had protected me as best he could. He was a thread of hope to me because he always stood up to my father. I don't know how he didn't die from the punishments he got. I was brave too, but I knew my limitations. Gerry didn't. He never gave up. He ran like a hare for us. Now they were taking him away, as if he was the problem, leaving me to the maniac, my father. I felt complete despair.'

As she watched, her father stormed into the house, thumping all round him as he raved about this outrage against his parental rights. 'We were terrified in the house,' she recalled. 'He was lashing out at us.'

McColgan demanded that a pencil be found, and when he got it, thundered out to the gate, where he signed something on the pier. 'He always had this thing that if you wrote something in pencil it didn't really count,' said Sophia. However, social worker Val O'Kelly and Garda Dave McDonald left the house at Cloonacurra with Joseph McColgan's permission to take Gerry McColgan into care. Sergeant O'Brien had already advised Mrs O'Kelly that in his view there were sufficient grounds to make a place of safety order, enabling them to take Gerry out of the home without parental permission in the event that McColgan refused.

Along with her grief, Sophia felt a twinge of optimism. 'In a way, I felt Gerry was being punished, but in another way, I felt that just maybe he was being rescued and I knew he would try and get help for the rest of us. I began to hope and pray that the social workers would soon be back for me and I would be saved as well.'

But there was a more ominous feeling too. 'I felt a huge responsibility descending onto my shoulders. Gerry had been the eldest, the strong one. He'd taken the brunt of the violence. Now he was gone. I knew that I would have to take his place.' That night, her father would prove her right. 'He came to me and he was jeering at me. He said, "You're for it now. You've nobody to protect you. You're all mine. I can do what I want with you from now on." I thought I'd never see Gerry again.' Her father battered her fiercely that night. After he left her, she cried herself to sleep, alone now in the room she had shared with her brother.

Sophia also had to watch her mother being kicked and beaten that evening. 'He used the boots,' said Sophia. Patsy was pregnant again, though that did not stop her husband expecting her to labour and farm. Sophia was carrying a lot of the weight of the housework as well as caring for the little ones. There were five children. 'I'd have to fold the blankets, put them away, sweep the floor, watch the fire and cook the dinner. I was constantly changing nappies over those years, and washing them in a bucket with bleach. When a baby cried, and babies are always crying, I'd get beaten, and badly beaten. The sexual violence got far, far worse, too, after Gerry was taken away.'

The risk of death or injury from accidents caused by McColgan's recklessness was high. The family used to be crammed into the tiny cab of the tractor, babies and all. Sophia remembers being brought in this way into quarries and other dangerous places. 'What must people have thought who saw us? They must have wondered what sort of a man would bring his family to such places.' She remembers an accident one day when her father brought her down a narrow road near the sea. 'It was raining and we were beside the sea and the road was all slippery. The bike suddenly went from under him and I was thrown onto the road.'

While Sophia's sufferings were increasing at home, there were stirrings of concern for her in the outside world. Phyllis Kilcoyne, then known as Sister Colette, was principal of Coláiste Mhuire in Ballymote, at which Gerry had been enrolled in September 1982. She was an experienced guidance counsellor. She had met

McColgan when he barged in with his wife after Gerry's first term, demanding a school report. Sister Colette recalled that McColgan's aggressive behaviour towards his wife on that occasion caused her to fear for Patsy McColgan's safety. It also made her decide that she would never meet this man on her own. In her statement to Gardaí in 1993, Sister Colette described McColgan as 'very articulate and very intimidating'.

A few months after the confrontation about the report, towards the end of May, Gerry fell asleep in class and was sent to see the principal. Sister Colette told the High Court that she remembered the child standing in the doorway of her office 'crying desperately'. He told her about having been beaten by his father, and when she offered to take him home, said this would lead to another beating. The following morning she talked with him for more than an hour. 'He told me he had been beaten by his father, that he had been stripped naked and beaten. I remember that he told me about a cement block on his fingers and that his arm had been broken,' she told the court. 'In particular, I remember still the ache of his cry as he told me about his fear for Sophia, his younger sister.'

Sister Colette was appalled, but became even more disturbed when Gerry said something about photographs. 'That rang alarm bells for me,' she said. 'I instinctively felt that because of the stripping naked and because of his concern for Sophia, I suspected sexual abuse.' She said that Gerry cried differently when he spoke about his sister. 'My memory of him about Sophia was him crying very painfully and achefully as he said he was fearful for Sophia.' Sister Colette decided the children needed help. She rang the Health Board. 'My memory is . . . I think what I first heard was that there had been a file on the McColgan family, but that it was now closed,' she said. Social worker Bridie Hughes undertook to come to the school and look into the matter. She did so, and it is not known what action the Health Board would or would not have taken following this, because events overtook it.

Sister Colette did not at that stage know that Gerry had also that week confided in Father Burns, a priest who had conducted a retreat at the school. He had also spoken to one of his teachers, Mrs Candon, to whom he had shown a bruise on his hip caused by a beating. Since it was the end of the school year, Mrs Candon told him that if anything happened during the holidays, he could come to her. That weekend, he did so, running almost six miles across the fields to her house to tell her he had been beaten again. Mrs Candon brought the boy to Sergeant O'Brien, and the social work department was once again called in. Sergeant O'Brien advised social worker Val O'Kelly that he believed McGolgan to be potentially dangerous, and when Mrs O'Kelly went to the house at Cloonacurra she was accompanied by Garda McDonald.

When Sister Colette was invited to a case conference on 9 June 1983, she decided to bring a delegation. Two priests, along with Mrs Candon and herself, attended the conference at Markievicz House. They were not happy about what happened there. 'The view of Gerry's behaviour at that time was that he was somebody who needed to be disciplined rather than as somebody who seemed to need to be heard,' Sister Colette told the High Court. 'We were not listened to, in the sense that the allegations needed to be checked out and that there was a crisis in the family. "Discipline" is the word I heard from the conference.' Sister Colette said she had come away from the conference uneasy. 'I still carry that unease to this day,' she said in court. She and her colleagues had one very particular worry. 'My concern was that Gerard's other statement about his concern for Sophia wasn't heard,' she said.

It was Dr Moran who told the case conference that Gerry needed discipline. According to the record kept by the Board, the doctor said that the boy was manipulative and that he 'would not recommend the soft option of care elsewhere . . . [Gerry] needed hard discipline and oversight'. During the High Court case, Counsel for Dr Moran, Mr Hanratty, put it to Sister Colette that Dr Moran had with him at the case conference a psychologist's report from 1979 in which it was noted that Gerry had 'tried to manipulate' a test, but had 'responded to firm handling'. Mr Justice Johnson said that this did not demonstrate a finding that Gerry had a manipulative personality. Mr Hanratty replied, 'I did not say that, my Lord.' After the case, Dr Moran told reporters that some of his comments had been taken out of context. Val O'Kelly told the 1983 conference that during a visit to the McColgan home a few days previously, McColgan had admitted that he had ill-treated Gerry. Mrs O'Kelly said Mrs McColgan was dominated by her husband to the extent that she would side with him against the children. Recommending intensive social work with the family, Mrs O'Kelly said that in her view the McColgan children were at risk of non-accidental injury. The doctor who had examined Gerry on his reception into care had noted bruising, which had been 'inflicted with considerable force'. Mrs O'Kelly and Dr Moran were given key roles. It was agreed that Mrs O'Kelly was to maintain oversight of the situation, and any assaults were to be reported to Dr Moran, who would also try to advise Joe McColgan of 'the consequences of his actions'. The conference decided that while McColgan was violent towards his family, there was no basis for legal proceedings.

In care, at a group home called Geevagh in south-east County Sligo, Gerry soon began to talk. He revealed that he — and Sophia — had been sexually abused by their father. He was brought to Dr

Moran for an examination. The doctor, who was at the time seeing Gerry weekly for counselling, recorded that he found no physical evidence of such abuse. Dr Moran also confronted Joe McColgan with Gerry's allegation. Patsy, who was also present, became vehemently angry with Gerry, accusing him of lying. Gerry insisted that he was telling the truth, adding, 'He's at Sophia too.' Looking back, Patsy says that she was unable to believe her son.

In the drawing room upstairs, Dr Moran got the McColgans to swear on the Bible that there was no sexual abuse in their home. Val O'Kelly's recollection is that Dr Moran's plan to examine Sophia was thwarted when Patsy heard of it and told McColgan, who refused to allow it. However, Dr Moran has a record of examining Sophia in July 1983. Notes were read in the High Court indicating that she appeared to be '*virgo intacta*', with the unbroken hymen of a girl who has not had sexual intercourse. Sophia told the High Court that she found this record appalling and that the examination had never taken place. 'No one touched me down there in those parts of my body apart from my father,' she said. She had, by 1983, been raped for seven years.

Sophia remembers the night her parents came home after the showdown over Gerry's allegations at Dr Moran's. 'My father viciously attacked my mother. It was all her fault, he said. This was the son she had reared, she and her parents. He kicked her around the place. He got her to agree that she was to blame,' Sophia said. 'I knew that Gerry was telling the truth.' Looking back, Patsy feels that her perception of reality at that time was distorted. 'Joe McColgan had it embedded in me that Gerry told lies,' she said. 'I thought the sex abuse thing was something Gerry had dreamed up. I didn't believe him.'

Sophia did not talk to her mother about the fact that McColgan was raping her. 'I had no relationship with her,' she told the High

Court. 'My father broke those bonds. To this day we don't have a mother-daughter relationship. I remember asking her why my father was treating us all so badly, and she cried and said she did not know what had gone wrong, but we would just have to make the best of it.'

One person who knew the family at this time said that Patsy's personality appeared to have been completely subsumed into that of her tyrannical husband. She was incapable of siding with her children. 'It was as if he had extinguished her maternal instinct,' she said. Sophia's memory is that Patsy tried. She was kind when she could be, but it did not go further than that. When a child had retreated into frozen silence, Patsy would try to coax the little one back. 'She couldn't say she loved us, but sometimes when the violence was going on, she'd look at me with tears in her eyes and I'd know she loved me,' Sophia said. 'In a way, it was harder for her than for us. She had loved him. He had her like a spider has a fly in its web. He had sucked out her entrails and she was just a husk. She was hardly on this planet a lot of the time. She looked out through a wall of tears and all was darkness. We were children, and we had never loved him or expected anything of him except violence. My mother was a hostage.'

While Gerry was in care, he also told his Granny Sally that his father had sexually abused him. 'I didn't even think he knew the meaning of the word sexual,' she said in her statement to Gardaí in 1993. 'I just could not believe him, because he was very distraught and I thought he was just making it up.' Gerry also told a woman who lived in Ballinacarrow, but she did not believe him either.

When McColgan informed Sophia that he was sending her to the Ursuline Convent in Sligo, he claimed it was because five generations of McColgan girls had been educated there. 'I think it had more to do with what he wanted to do to me after school,' she said. In fact, the move represented a sudden change of plan. McColgan had previously enrolled his daughter at Coláiste Mhuire in Ballymote, just a few miles from Cloonacurra and connected by a school bus service. Not long after Gerry was taken into care, McColgan turned up at the school, unannounced and demanding to see Mrs Candon. During the High Court hearing, she recalled the meeting, at which Sister Colette and Patsy McColgan were present.

'We met in a very small office, perhaps nine feet by eight feet. Mr McColgan paced up and down and around it and ordered the women to sit down,' said Mrs Candon. Asked by Garret Cooney, Senior Counsel, if McColgan's manner was intimidating, she replied that it was. 'He kept repeating a phrase and the phrase was directed at me, and the phrase he kept repeating was "Why did you do it?"' In the public benches, Sophia and her family exchanged glances and laughed. Why did you do it? It was a question they remembered all too well. Mrs Candon said she took it that he meant why had she brought Gerry to the Gardaí earlier that year. She told him she would do it again if she had to, and that, she said, brought the meeting to a swift end.

Sister Colette cannot have been altogether surprised when Sophia did not turn up in September 1983. Coláiste Mhuire was clearly not a place to which Joe McColgan might safely send his children. During his cross-examination of Sister Colette in the High Court on 12 December 1997, Patrick Hanratty, Counsel for Dr Moran, asked, 'Would you agree with me that in those days the detection of the abuse of children was not a fine art, or as fine an art as it is today?' 'No, I wouldn't,' replied Sister Colette. She said that she and her staff were 'on alert' for signs of disturbance indicative of such abuse. Mr Hanratty put it to her that notwithstanding this, Gerry was, throughout his time at the school, being 'violently and continually abused by this father and it wasn't picked up'.

At this point, Mr Justice Johnson interjected. 'Sister, if you had known that there had been previous incidents or, at least, one previous incident of abuse to Gerry in the home, would you have looked differently on the symptoms he displayed?' he asked. Sister Colette did not hesitate. 'Yes,' she replied.

The then senior social worker, Mr Duffy, told me during an interview for this book that the rule of confidentiality precluded the passing on of such information. 'Confidentiality meant to social workers that any information they received almost fell within the seal of the confessional,' he said. No one had contacted Sister Colette at any stage to indicate that there was a history of suspected non-accidental injury to the McColgan children and, after the case conference in June 1983, no one contacted her again. She was not asked to pass on any records to Gerry's next school, and she was not told that Sophia had been enrolled elsewhere.

6

'I WAS SO,
SO DIFFERENT'

The day he put his daughter's name down for the Ursuline Convent, Joe McColgan bought Sophia the brown school uniform, then brought her home on the old Honda 50 he had just acquired. 'He was driving like a lunatic on the way home, crossing over the white line and in front of traffic and back again, laughing all the time,' said Sophia. 'I was terrified. Suddenly, whatever happened, we skidded and my right ankle went into the back wheel of the bike, which sheared it. My shoes were destroyed and my foot was ruined. It still hurts even all these years later. It is still not right.' McColgan brought her home and ordered Patsy to bandage the foot. But the bleeding would not stop. While Patsy attended to the injury, McColgan was shouting at Sophia, blaming her for the accident. Eventually, he gave her a beating, put her on the motorbike and drove her back to Sligo, to the casualty department at the hospital. 'He told me to tell them I had tripped over a stone at school,' she said. A month later, she was brought to casualty with a burned eye.

'I was like a robot,' she said. 'I was so terrified all the time. Every day was a huge struggle. My father had been using such militaristic tactics on me for so many years that by the time I got to secondary school, you can easily imagine I was somebody who couldn't speak. I really think I had a disability. I think I had lost the power to speak. I was soft-spoken and I only spoke if it was necessary. According to him, everything I said was wrong. I had very little confidence about what I said. I was afraid people would think it was wrong and reject me.'

Still forbidden to make friends, Sophia was inevitably isolated. To reinforce that, her father would arrive back at school at lunch-time to ensure that she was not speaking to anyone. She sat alone and silent. By this stage, the dapper Joe McColgan, who had returned from England with his dickie bows and fancy shoes, had let things slip. 'He had let himself go completely,' said Sophia. 'He would dress in rags, dirty old overalls and wellingtons, and he had put on a load of weight. Once he had us in the cottage with him in control, he no longer felt he needed to put up a front any more. He would still dress up to go and see Dr Moran, but not to the same extent. He would turn up at the Ursuline covered in muck, just to humiliate me. But he was still fit and strong from walking the lands at Killerry.'

Sophia did her best to appear normal at school. 'I tried to pretend to be like the other girls, because I didn't want them to think I was so weird and different from them, which I was. I was so, so different. I didn't want them to know what was happening to me at home.' She was already at a disadvantage, because her family was poorer than those of most of the other girls at the Ursuline.

The school had been set up in 1850. The then Bishop of Elphin, Dr Browne, had been so impressed by the Ursuline Sisters' 'peculiar talent for the training of pupils of the higher class' at their convent in Galway that he invited them to set up a school in Sligo. The founding sisters aimed to inculcate 'elevation of character, goodness of heart and grace of manner'. In the 1920s the school prospectus advertised that 'no pains are spared to mould practical virtues which make home happy and are the best result and reward of a Christian education'.

Starting in September 1983, McColgan would drive his Honda 50, or (worse), his ancient tractor, up through the grounds, past the statue of St Joseph casting benign eyes on a little child, to leave Sophia in, and to collect her. 'The other girls laughed at me,' she said. 'They all came in cars. It was a posh school.' McColgan was consistently late bringing his daughter to school, and she would have to make an entrance on her own and make her excuses to teachers who were irritated by the interruption of their class.

Some of the girls made fun of me constantly. There was one girl in particular. My father used to make me wear this old coat he had bought in a second-hand shop called Clancy's. The coat was brutal. It was dark brown, all big flaps and big, old buttons. It was out of fashion by centuries. One day, this girl was making fun of the coat to her friends and I decided to teach her a lesson. She really had nothing to jeer about herself — she was fat. I shouldn't say that — my Granny Sally and Grandad Michael always taught us that you shouldn't look down on anyone less fortunate than yourself, that you should try to help them.

Anyway, this day I walked past her and her friends and there was a hush and then a big laugh as I went by. We had these swing doors like hospital doors in the school and I waited on the far side of these and I could hear every word they were saying about me. I was so hurt. I thought, I can never be the same as them. I am totally trapped, and if I make a move, somebody at home will be killed. My father had made huge threats about what he'd do to Michelle if I ever tried to leave.

I sat behind these double doors, desperately trying to work out what I would say. I said to myself, think, Sophia, think. The big girl was really letting me have it and the others were enjoying it. I decided to sit there and wait and see did she have any insight. She came through the doors. The first thing they all used to say when they saw me was, 'Hi, Sophia.' I looked at her. I glared at her. I literally bored my eyes into her. She went red, and red and red. She said in a shaky voice, 'Hi, Sophia,' and she walked on. Then I waited for her friends. They said, 'Hi, Sophia, uhhh . . .'

They did feel ashamed. The next day the big girl came to me and said she was sorry. I quoted a priest back to her, 'You can take a person's character away, like tearing a piece of A4 paper,' I said. 'You might sellotape it back together but you'll never make it the same as before you did it.' I think in all her young years she had never heard anything like it. I suppose I was kind of weird. But things like that really hurt me. It was my way of explaining to her what she had done. I felt that if she learned a lesson she wouldn't let it happen again in years to come. She wouldn't let her own children do it. She'd stop them.

Sophia remembers spending a day in the infirmary, sick. A nun brought her tea. She remembers long corridors. She has a strange memory from this time, of a day when, after her father picked her up at the convent, he brought her on the tractor to Drumcliff. He had to pick up an old fridge and other junk he had bought. When they got to Drumcliff, he stopped the tractor at the graveyard. He brought her under the old sycamore trees to show her W. B. Yeats's grave. He read out the epitaph:

'Cast a cold eye,
on life, on death.
Horseman, pass by!'

'He recalled Yeats's coffin passing through the streets of Sligo when he was a boy,' she said. 'At times I think he had an appreciation of art and culture. He told me he had been good at art. He said he was harshly treated by the Marist Brothers — they ran the national school he went to. He said he was beaten and he used to wet himself with fear.'

After this interlude 'under bare Ben Bulben's head' at Drumcliff churchyard, McColgan brought his daughter to a café, where he ordered tea and Club milk biscuits. 'It was most unusual,' she said. However, on the way home, something fell off the trailer, which he had loaded carelessly, and Sophia was beaten for it when she got home.

Every day at secondary school brought fresh evidence to thirteen-year-old Sophia of just how drastically different her life was from the lives of her contemporaries. 'I started to learn the facts of life,' she said. 'Not in the abusive way my father had taught me. They showed us a film in religion class at the Ursuline. I think it was called "The Miracle of Life". I watched it and I thought it was fascinating and beautiful and every good thing that my life was not. I began to look around. I didn't have what the other girls had. They went to basketball in the evenings, or to visit each other at their homes, and then they had a curfew of maybe nine o'clock or whatever when they had to be home. I had no friends. I hadn't a normal father, a normal family, a normal life.'

One of the teachers at the Ursuline at this time remembers Sophia as 'a lovely girl, very sweet and ladylike and polite, not a bit rebellious'. The staff were aware that she was the butt of jokes from other girls, the teacher said. She saw Sophia as a loner. McColgan and his wife used to come to parent-teacher meetings at the school. 'He used to irritate people, because he'd take over. I knew his own family since I was a child. They were very decent, respectable people. The father used to call his wife, "Mammy" and she would call him "Daddy". Joe McColgan did that too. He'd be full of concern for Sophia, and later on for Michelle too when she came to the Ursuline. His wife, Patsy, would say something and he'd say, "You shut up, Mammy," and he'd make as if to hit her. But it was all just a friendly gesture, we thought. Another person who met McColgan and his wife around this time remembers that when Patsy would venture an opinion, her husband would shout, 'Leave the talking to me, woman.'

During this period, McColgan was attending Dr Moran for counselling. There were, according to Dr Moran's lawyers, thirty-eight sessions between the case conference, after Gerry was taken into care in June 1983, and the following April. Dr Moran's Counsel said in the High Court that he did not take notes of what was said at these sessions.

There was kindness as well as cruelty for Sophia at the Ursuline. One teacher in particular seemed to pay attention to the strange, silent little country girl with long hair and big eyes full of trouble. 'My biology teacher was lovely,' said Sophia. 'She encouraged me to answer questions in class. I developed a love of science because of her. At that time, there was no one in my house to encourage me. Granny Sally poured love on me. She didn't need to say anything. The fact that she was there was a comfort. I felt she loved me as she had promised she always would. But if I saw her once a week I was lucky.

'This lady would always encourage me. I was shy and I did not say much. She would say, "Well, Sophia, what do you think about the nodules on the clover plant?" She would have been explaining about the conversion of nitrogen in the soil, and how the bacteria that grow in the roots of clover are of great benefit to other plants. I told her that I thought it was fantastic. I said I thought it was great this relationship of symbiosis, a wonderful thing. I thought it would be nice if there was a lot of things out there that worked in such harmony, not detrimental to each other but of benefit to something else. I think she understood that there was something wrong with me.'

Patsy remembers an occasion around this time when she asked Sophia if she would mind doing something for her. 'He turned round and said to Sophia, "Don't do anything for that one, she's not worth dirtying your hands for."'

Sophia remembers that Patsy was being kicked around incessantly. 'He was always particularly violent to Mammy when she was pregnant. This time, she nearly lost her baby,' she said. 'She lost blood. I saw her haemorrhaging through a chair onto the floor. She was shaking a lot. I thought she was going to die. He turned around and said once she was out of the way what he wouldn't do to me. You can imagine how terrifying that was. Gerry was away. I was losing all the blocks I needed between me and his violence. Useless and all as my mother was when it came to stopping my father, at least her being there was some kind of protection. The night she went into hospital to have the baby, he took me into her bed and he raped me ferociously.'

Gerry was increasingly often out for weekends. He stayed with Sally and Michael, but also came to Cloonacurra. Val O'Kelly had noted that he seemed to have a 'pathological need' to be with his family and that he needed to be rehabilitated. 'We used to have to sit like dummies when Gerry was in the house,' said Sophia. 'We weren't allowed to talk to him. I remember my father treating him really badly during that time. He spent a lot of time alone with Gerry, interrogating him. It was all very hush hush.' Her description of how McColgan brainwashed his victims into seeing things his way indicates just how strenuous a process it was: 'He would have been twisting his thoughts and making him change his mind about what he said. He would have been telling him what he should be saying rather than what he did tell.' She remembers that Gerry was made to sign something, though she was not aware at the time what it was. Early in 1984, Gerry informed social workers that he was withdrawing his allegations of sexual abuse against his father. He said he would deal with McColgan in his own way.

Gerry would later tell them that his father had made him retract. In April 1984 he told Mrs O'Kelly that his father was still sexually abusing him and had done so a few days previously during a visit home. Mrs O'Kelly was deeply worried. The last time she had attempted to visit the house at Cloonacurra, McColgan had met her at the gate brandishing a shovel and threatening to set his dogs on her if she didn't go away and leave his family alone. When she reported back to her senior, Mr Duffy, he was alarmed at the potential risk that McColgan would carry out his threats of violence. He told her that in the light of McColgan's physically threatening behaviour towards her, she was not to return to the house at Cloonacurra.

Convinced that the situation was at crisis point, Mrs O'Kelly wrote a strongly worded report, which made several recommendations. Chief among these was that legal action should be taken to remove either the McColgan children or their father from the family home. She expressed the view that the children could not be protected using a voluntary 'reception-into-care' option. She said that Gerry now accepted that he could not go home, and that he had expressed concern for his siblings, particularly Sophia. Mrs O'Kelly wrote:

It is my opinion that I am dealing with a very pathological family. The degree of abuse both physical and sexual is at an extraordinarily high level . . . Joseph McColgan is an extremely sick man . . . and seriously perverted sexually. I feel he has everyone terrorised and keeps control by terrorising. His personality disorder is such that he could not be considered a fit parent. His sexual activities regarding the children can only be called criminal.

Noting that 'one of the most significant pieces of evidence' she had was that McColgan had never denied the allegations which had been made against him, Ms O'Kelly said corroborative evidence should be sought from Sophia; she commented that Dr Moran had attempted to do this, but that Patsy McColgan forcefully denied that the allegations against her husband were true. Mrs O'Kelly said she was sure that Sophia was very frightened, and that safeguards for her protection would have to be initiated. She stated that if her recommendation was not followed through by the case conference, her position as social worker to the family would be 'untenable'. She added that, while she felt strongly about what she was saying, she realised that there was a 'slight possibility' that she was wrong. She concluded that, 'only time and subsequent events will determine that'.

The report is a remarkable document. The North Western Health Board knew in April 1984, through its social worker, that

Joseph McColgan was in all likelihood a highly dangerous, violent paedophile. It knew that he had a record of injuring his children, to the extent that they had had to attend the casualty department of its hospital. It knew that he had total control over a household in which a battered woman was living with five children, at least one of whom it had reason to believe was being sexually abused. Its social worker was recommending urgent action.

There appears to be no record of the case conference anticipated by Mrs O'Kelly. Decisions were taken which were to have drastic consequences for Patsy McColgan and her children, but they are not recorded. Mrs O'Kelly told me a conference did take place. 'It made several decisions,' she said. 'We decided to get the family to see Dr Tony Carroll's team in Galway. They were developing family therapy there. And we decided to seek legal advice.' Mrs O'Kelly said that an appointment was made for the McColgans with the family therapy team but the family did not keep it. Instead the professionals used the opportunity to discuss the case. 'I felt at that time that I had failed miserably,' said Mrs O'Kelly. 'I felt to blame. What I took from the psychologist's advice was that I appeared to have become a threat to McColgan and that we would have to seek an opportunity to re-engage with the family.' She and Mr Duffy had a meeting with the Board's solicitor, Declan Hegarty, on 15 April 1984. Mrs O'Kelly said she sent the lawyer copies of reports on the family dating back to 1983 and including the one she wrote in April 1984.

On 9 December 1997, in the High Court, John Rogers put it to Sophia that his clients, the NWHB, could not have acted differently. 'I think, Sophia, we all have a different knowledge of these problems now,' he said. 'But in 1983 when the principal witness says: "I withdraw the allegations" and it is recorded that he did say so, do you not accept that it was a great problem for my clients?' Sophia agreed.

Mr Rogers went on:

You see, at that time, I don't want to trouble you with lawyers, but on 15 April 1984, there was a meeting between the social worker, a Mr Hegarty, a solicitor in Sligo, and the senior social worker with a view to establishing what could be done in this case and the legal advice was that the evidence wasn't good enough. Do you see what I mean, Sophia? We had a problem. We were caught in a loop that we couldn't get out of, even though we wanted to . . . There wasn't enough evidence to protect either Gerard or you.

'There wasn't enough investigation,' countered Sophia.

Asked by Mr Hanratty if she had herself suspected abuse of her other siblings, Sophia said, 'You don't understand. I was thirteen years of age. I was a child trying to go through adolescence with a monster of a father abusing me. You don't understand. I was not able.'

Mrs O'Kelly continued to hold the view that although Gerry needed family contact, he could not go home while there was a risk of sexual abuse. However, Gerry took matters into his own hands and left the Health Board's home at Geevagh. He moved in with his mother's parents where he would stay until he left Ireland to seek work in England in 1986. Mrs O'Kelly told me that she believes that some of the actions she recommended in April 1984 were not legally possible at that time.

On 23 May 1984, Mr Duffy wrote to McColgan, enclosing a letter which had arrived for Gerry and telling McColgan that he could arrange to pick up the boy's belongings from Geevagh. 'Dear

Mr McColgan,' wrote Mr Duffy. 'Now that Gerard has returned home, I trust that he is settled and that things are working out for him satisfactorily. I enclose a letter addressed to Gerard and marked "private" which was received at Geevagh so that it may be delivered to him . . .' Mr Duffy invited McColgan to seek his assistance if he felt he needed it at any time. The McColgan file would effectively remain closed until 21 June 1993, when Michelle McColgan, then aged twenty-one, revealed that her father had raped, beaten and attempted to kill her repeatedly for approximately fifteen years.

7

'I WAS LIKE
ALICE IN WONDERLAND'

⁂

The boatman who takes tourists around Lough Gill, which straddles the borders of Sligo and Leitrim, steers in close to the shore at the foot of Killerry Mountain, to a tiny wooded island. His passengers rise with their cameras as he tells them that this is William Butler Yeats's 'The Lake Isle of Innisfree', about which the poet imagined,

'And I shall have some peace there, for peace comes dropping slow . . .'

A little further along the shore, the boatman indicates Slish Wood, known to Yeats as Sleuth Wood in his 'The Stolen Child'.

It was to Killerry that Joseph McColgan brought his children over the years, to his derelict stone house and its lands. 'It was a beautiful wilderness,' said Sophia. 'You could scream and scream your heart out and there wasn't a soul to hear you.'

Teachers at the Ursuline knew from Sophia that, after school, she had to go to the mountain with her father to look after the cattle. McColgan would collect her at 4.00 p.m. on the Honda

50, or sometimes on his tractor, and bring her to his parents' house on Circular Road. 'That was a very bleak house,' Sophia remembers.

> There was a long corridor with a living room, a kitchen and a back scullery. My grandfather would be sitting in the kitchen listening to the wireless, as he called it. My aunt would be in the living room. She would sit there with her head on her hand, looking out the window, bored. My grandmother would be working in the scullery.
>
> She was a very stern and paranoid sort of person. One day I was there, someone came to the door, a neighbour, and my grandmother made me hide with her under the window-sill until the visitor went away. She was disturbed, really. She used to be always going on at me about how a lady should behave. 'Keep your legs crossed. Be reserved. Don't speak till you're spoken to. Listen, Don't yap. Hold your head up high. Don't wear short dresses. Keep yourself right morally. Don't open the door to a stranger.' She was very old-fashioned. She was a scary woman really.
>
> Sometimes you would see a softness in her, you'd see a different woman, one who had undergone years and years of living with a strict man with strange ways. She lived her life for a man. She was a servant to a man, and she was badly treated by him. He was viciously strict. They both believed in punishing children. My father had a terrible childhood. Once his father left him for days with a broken leg before bringing him to hospital, so you can see where my father got that idea. My grandmother had to serve her husband his dinner and his tea, and she even used to wash his hair. She had a sad life and sometimes she seemed almost like a child,

vulnerable, just wanting someone to be nice to her and look after her. She had no life of her own, though she had some sort of diploma. There was a picture of her in the house holding a diploma. My father was always showing it to me.

My father was a total failure. His father had let him know that from an early age. Several of his brothers had professional jobs. He had no gift for anything. He couldn't really read or write. He was a rejected child, in a way. My grandparents were terribly stuck up. My grandmother thought she was too good for most people. They thought they were somebodies and most other people were nobodies. My grandfather was one of the first men in Sligo to have a car. Yet they were poor, too. It is strange. My father said he had no shoes when he went to school. The attachment between him and his mother was frightening. When she died, he was absolutely grief stricken. He made me kiss her cold face in the morgue. I didn't want to. I didn't feel love for her, the way I loved my other Granny.

There was no welcome in the house in Circular Road, and Sophia, who would have left home at 8.00 in the morning and had meagre sandwiches for lunch, might not even be offered a cup of tea. She watched television, childish programmes for younger children, like 'Bosco'. 'Anything to keep my mind off the abuse,' she said. Other times, she remembers sitting outside the house, waiting for her father. She would pluck the tiny white petals off a daisy, reciting, 'Tinker, tailor, soldier, sailor/Rich man, poor man, beggar man, thief.' 'In my child's mind it was just a game, wondering who would I end up with. Who would marry me and make me happy?' They would spend an hour or two there. 'Then he'd say, "Come on, we'll go up the mountain on the way home and check the animals."' Nobody but Sophia knew what her father really made her do on the mountain, almost every day. The journey would be filled with dread.

The house is old and effectively derelict, grey stone against the grey stone of the mountain, a desolate place. 'He'd leave the motorbike or the tractor at the end of the lane and I would have to walk up to the house. I had to. Everything I did at that house was done against my will. I did nothing with him voluntarily.'

We got to the mountain house. The doors were small, only about three-quarters of the height of doors you'd get now. In the house there was a small staircase. He used to make me go up the stairs. There was a small door on the left at the top. There was a lift-up latch. You would go in and close the door behind you.

Inside, there was a small room with a small window with four panes. You could see the land. There was a fireplace. A lot of the mortar was gone off the walls and you could see the wooden rafters and the slates of the roof. There was a chest in the room, like an old treasure chest. The metal on it was rusted and the wood had woodworm. I never looked in it to see what was inside. There was a thin mattress for a single bed on the floor.

In the room, my father made me take off my school uniform. I had to fold it and make sure no dust got on it. I had to put it on a bag. He did not want any evidence brought home. He didn't want my mother asking any questions. If there was dust on it he would beat me. Then I had to lie down on the mattress. He would lie on top of me, and he would rape me.

To start off with, the rapes were very bad. I felt great pain. The pain was excruciating. If someone stuck a knife into my body and the blood poured out, that is how painful they were. I have an incredibly high pain threshold now. I often burn myself accidentally and I don't even notice. It amazes me how much pain I can take, even when I was giving birth. I have endured so much, it has made me strong.

However, at the time, Sophia found her father's violence intolerable. She would scream and cry and she was deeply traumatised. 'I couldn't handle it.' She began to try to think of ways to stop her father bringing her to the mountain. She would get out her books at the house on Circular Road and start on her homework, delaying departure. But it did not work. All that happened was that her father kept her even later at Killerry. Sometimes, there would be shopping to be done on the way. Sophia would be left standing by the motorbike, come rain, hail or snow, while her father went about his business. 'I was always so guarded by him,' she said. 'He might stop somewhere to get some item for an engine, and I'd be left with the helmet on at the bike, while he'd be inside talking. He was fascinated by engines and how things worked. Given the chance, he might have been a brilliant engineer. I used to be mortified. There'd be lads covered in oil and grease as black as the ace of spades coming and going from the workshop and there was this girl standing there motionless for hours on end. I couldn't move because he'd be watching. I guess he was afraid maybe someone would talk to me and gain my confidence.'

Once, she recalls, outside a shop in Sligo, a man came over and gave her a Twix chocolate bar. She refused it, but he insisted, so eventually she took it and ate it hungrily. When her father returned, he had seen what happened, demanding to know why she had broken the rule of never talking to strangers. 'He said, "Haven't I told you it is dangerous to take sweets from someone you don't know?" And then he took me up the mountain and raped me.'

Another day, he came out of a supermarket with a large load of tins of beans which had been going cheap. He had bought no other items, although this was the weekly shopping. He piled them into tomato boxes and stacked them up high behind Sophia. But when he went to leave, the overloaded motorbike slipped and broke the large plate glass window of the store. 'The security man came, very angry, and ordered my father up to the manager's office,' Sophia said. 'The manager started out wanting to know what my father was going to do about the fact that he'd broken the window, but my father just turned on him. He said, "Who do you think you are? Do you know who you are talking to, you pup, there in your suit and you hardly out of nappies . . ." And he went on and on about how he could get the manager into all sorts of trouble because of this dangerous window he had which was a risk to children. He said I was there as his witness and of course I had to say, "Yes." It was so embarrassing. The manager was a lovely man, a gentleman. By the end of this interview, he was sort of apologising to my father, and telling him he was very sorry to have troubled him. My father was so intimidating. I was mortified.'

Up on the mountain, Sophia had to do exactly what her father demanded. If she failed to stimulate him, he made her have oral sex. He made her kiss him. He made her put her tongue in his mouth. He buggered her. He made her watch as he raped her in front of an old broken mirror he brought to the mountain. He used condoms, and re-used them repeatedly, using elastic bands to hold them on. He inserted spermicide into Sophia, using a large cattle syringe. He douched her with disinfectant. He beat her if she did not comply with his orders. 'He butchered me,' she said. 'Often with his weight on me, I couldn't breathe.'

The sexual violence might last for three hours or more. Then there might be work to be done on the land. Later Sophia would have to get back on the motorbike for the hazardous drive back down the mountain and across the windy roads to Cloonacurra. 'It could be ten o'clock or later by the time we got to the cottage,' she said. 'I'd look in the pot and see what was left for me to eat. It mightn't be much, or it mightn't be anything at all. My mother would try to get something for me, but my father always expected that whatever was there was for him. Then I'd do my homework.'

When she was not at school, or being raped on the mountain, Sophia was, along with her mother and her siblings, working for McColgan. While her mother laboured outside, Sophia would look after the house and mind the little ones. By this time, there were six children in the family. (The two youngest members of the family have requested that their names should not be mentioned.) One evening, in a repeat of the earlier incident when Sophia was accused of almost killing Michelle, one of the small children had an accident out at the back of the house, which was littered with bits of old cars and rubbish which McColgan had accumulated. 'My father came in roaring and shouting that I had killed my sister and he made me put up all the old cloths that we had as curtains as if there was a death in the family,' said Sophia. 'He had me terrified that I was to blame for my sister dying. He took her to the hospital, but she didn't even need treatment.'

Real injuries, those caused by McColgan himself, were not treated with any urgency, and some were not treated at all. Sophia remembers a night that Michelle had been up on the mountain with her father. When they came home, and she took the motorbike helmet off, she was shaking and pale and her head was covered in blood from a wound which was still bleeding. 'Mammy cleaned up the wound, but she could see it was bad and she begged my father to bring Michelle to the doctor. He said that Michelle would be fine. He said she was stupid — she'd been standing in the wrong place and a spanner had fallen on her,' said Sophia.

The night Sophia started to menstruate, her parents were out; she had been left in charge, and a fire broke out in the house. The place was full of smoke after clothes which had been left to dry on a pipe started to melt and burn. Neighbours had to come to help. When McColgan arrived home later, he took Sophia into a room on her own, found out she was menstruating and proceeded to bring her out and humiliate her in front of her mother. 'He also beat and kicked me stupid round the house,' said Sophia.

McColgan kept his children in a constant state of terror. 'He would make us watch horror films on television,' said Sophia. 'There was one about a man who was killing people for their blood. He also liked ones with people in mental hospitals. He'd tell us that that is what would happen to us if we ever told anyone about what went on in our house. He said we would end up in a mental hospital and we would get electric shock treatment and we'd never see Mammy or our brothers and sisters again. He would threaten to kill me with a knife too. And he would beat Mammy too if you went against him in any way.'

All her life, Sophia had been trying to find a way to escape from her brutal father. At first, she had assumed that adults would save her. Not her mother — she knew her mother had been broken. Not her maternal grandmother — her father had ensured that Sally knew that any move she made would result in further violence for Patsy or the children. Sophia had seen people bring Gerry back to his father after he'd run and run for help. She had been sent home from hospital. Her father had been brought to court, and let go. Now Gerry had been taken away.

'I waited and waited for them to come for the rest of us,' said Sophia. 'I felt that if they believed Gerry, they would surely not have let my father have access to the other children. I thought, if they are doing this to save Gerry, they will surely save all of us. When that did not happen, the way it looked to me was that Gerry had been taken out because he was seen as the problem. It was a way of silencing what was going on in the family, putting out the flame, but not looking for the cause of the fire. But I did know that Val O'Kelly believed Gerry and was concerned for him. I was dying for her to come and take me out and talk to me as well. But she did not come.'

After the High Court case was settled, and the lawyers, stenographers, journalists and on-lookers had left, Mrs O'Kelly approached Sophia, who had stayed behind in the silent courtroom. 'She put her hand on my arm and she said, "Lookit, Sophia, I tried to reach you all those years back and I think you were trying to reach me too, but we never succeeded." She said she did come to the Ursuline. I know she did her best, and I will never hold anything against Val O'Kelly because of that. Others were to blame. But that didn't stop me as a child just feeling totally abandoned. I had been left to fend for myself with a maniac of a father, left for him eventually to kill me in his mission of whatever he needed to do to make himself feel confident. I felt so hurt. It is all right for an adult to say they were trying to reach a child, but how was a child to reach an adult? I had the huge disadvantage of being a child. I was the one with the monster in my face twenty-four hours a day. The way the authorities treated me was panic and fuss for a short time and then nothing. A total nothing.'

Interviewed for this book, in a personal capacity, Mrs O'Kelly confirms that she went to the Ursuline Convent in May 1984.

Sophia today.

Sophia in her pram at less than two years of age. The photograph was taken at Ballinacarrow.

Sophia as a toddler playing at Ballinacarrow.

First Communion, 1976.

Sophia (centre) at her First Communion party.

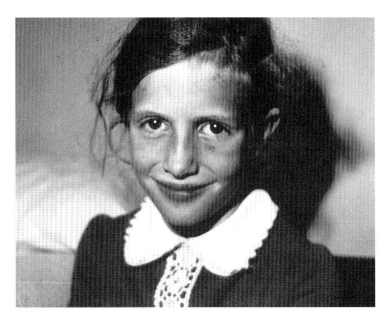

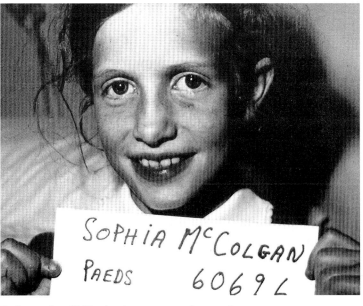

SOPHIA McCOLGAN
PAEDS   6069 L

In hospital in 1979 after her nose was fractured.

Sophia's grandfather in Ballinacarrow Church, June 1994.

Sophia photographed with her grandmother at Sligo RTC on 6 November 1993. She has just been conferred with a B.Sc. (Hons) degree in Environmental Science and Technology.

Sophia as a student in one of the research laboratories in Sligo Regional Technical College, 1989-90. She was a first-year B.Sc. student at the time. A colour version of this photograph later appeared on the cover of Technology Ireland.

Sophia at Lough Gill with the Island of Innisfree in the background.

I had been trying to reach Sophia before that. I'd spoken with her grandmother in Ballinacarrow and I tried to organise that I would bring Sophia to visit Gerry at Geevagh, so that she and I could be alone. But Joe McColgan was very adept at keeping me away from Sophia. My last attempt to help was when I went to see the then head of the Ursuline (now the order's superior), Sister Mary Gilbride. I told Sister Gilbride that I thought Sophia was under stress at home, and she might show signs of that, and asked her to look out for it. I said the family had a lot of problems and I had been working with them. I didn't mention abuse. I didn't feel I could say any more. I felt I was leaving a door open. After all, Gerry had presented, that is, spoken about his abuse, at school. I thought Sophia might do the same. I didn't ask to see Sophia because I feared that McColgan would find out and make things worse for her. I didn't want to push too hard.

Mrs O'Kelly said she could see how Sophia felt abandoned. However, she added, 'I believed I had done all I could.'

An adolescent by this stage, and beginning to recognise how utterly abnormal her family was, Sophia began to be very angry. 'I just couldn't believe how my father was protected. His little environment was secured. Things got better for him rather than worse. Over the years the attitude seemed to be that if my mother got the children disciplined he wouldn't be upset. It sickens me that they were so concerned about how upset he was. There didn't seem to be any real recognition of what it must be like to have to live with such a man. I could have told about my pain and suffering if I had been helped, brought to a safe place and encouraged to talk. But as it was, I was so terrified and brutalised that I was caught in a world of silence. I realised when I was thirteen that no help was coming.'

Sophia began to use what she was learning in class to understand her situation. And she began to think about things she remembered her great-grandmother saying about the power of knowledge. 'It dawned on me that I had to do something to get the doctors and social workers and all the rest of them to listen to me and to believe me,' she said. 'I said to myself, "Sophia, you have to make them believe you. How? I'll become the same as them. I will get a degree. I will become a professional person. Then I will get somebody to do something about my father."' Looking back, she wonders what she might have done had she been able to make choices in the normal way. 'I might have decided to be a hairdresser, or a chef,' she said, 'something that appeals to normal teenagers. Instead I was under this terrible pressure. I had to get a degree.'

That was the long-term plan. In the meantime, Sophia had to find a way to cope with the daily violence. 'In the early times, when I got back from the mountain house, I'd find it very hard to concentrate. I would be looking at my books, but with the violence earlier in the evening I couldn't take anything in. I'd be sitting looking at the page for ages. I knew I would have to find some way to block it out.' Up on the mountain, she was to discover a remarkable technique to get her out of the place she calls 'the hell-hole'.

I felt so trapped and I wanted my freedom. I started to distance myself during the rapes. I found that I could leave my body. To start off with, I could see my body. I could see what was happening to it. I felt this yearning to be free. I finally escaped him, temporarily escaped him. I was able to leave the room, not through the door. It was as if there was no door. I walked down the path. Sometimes I would go and play with some little children in the fields. Often I went to a house near by. I made friends with this girl, an imaginary friend. She was the same age as me and she had a boyfriend. She was telling me all her problems. Her boyfriend wouldn't do this or do that for her — he was being a pain. She liked this other fellow and she broke it off with the old boyfriend.

Sophia laughed as she recalled some aspects of these memories within memories.

I don't think I went out with any of the lads I met in this dream, but I certainly went to discos. I definitely in my mind was doing all the things I wanted to do. At one stage in my dreams I was visiting my Great-Granny Mullen. I had a brilliant time. Then suddenly, I'd hear this voice from a great distance. It would be asking me questions about what was happening back in the room. I had to get back in a big hurry to my body. I rushed back and I was there and I woke up. I had to give an answer to my father, and usually it was, 'Yes.' Then I left again. It was a wonderful thing I was able to do.

I would close my eyes and dream. My body was there, but my heart and mind were gone. I was very skilled in that way as a child. I was like Alice in Wonderland, while my fifteen-stone father was on top of me raping me.

8

'PURE DETERMINED'

On a spring day in 1998, Sophia brought me to the mountain house at Killerry. We drove up a rutted, muddy lane on the side of the mountain, between banks starred with primroses. Sophia pointed out the corner on which her father had tried to run over Michelle on the motorbike five years previously. (It was this act of cruelty which brought about McColgan's downfall, when Michelle spoke out about it to a friend.) When she stopped the car, Sophia said, 'This is where he used to park the bike. I had to walk from here.' The beautiful wilderness she remembered was all around. The mountains and valleys of Sligo, Leitrim, Mayo and Fermanagh spread their colours about us. Skylarks whistled and flitted about over the bracken, and unseen corncrakes called in old meadows of farms long since abandoned. 'I love this environment,' said Sophia. 'I love knowing about all the plants and creatures in it, and the geography.' She bent her face towards the bright yellow flowers blazing on a whin bush. 'I love that smell, like coconut,' she said. 'I love the wildness of this place, this area. But it is so full of sadness and pain to me because of what he did to me here.'

Along the rough lane, strange objects began to appear. Huge broken metal cylinders lay rusting in a stream. Bits of old machinery jutted out of the bog. Oil drums, girders, an iron tractor seat. 'Look,' said Sophia, 'these are the stones he made us hoist up from the bottom of the mountain.' The stones were massive boulders, the size of a sheep. McColgan had decided to build a bridge over a stream, and it was his wife and children who had the impossible task of attempting to transform his grand plans into reality. 'I remember that rock there — there were four of us hoisting and pushing with a crowbar trying to get that one onto the low loader,' said Sophia, clambering down a bank to touch a jutting rock. 'Our hands used to be cut to pieces.'

Once the loader was full of stones, McColgan would get the children to cling onto the front of the tractor as a ballast against the weight of the stones, before setting off up the steep lane. Sophia remembers the tractor almost tipping backwards many times.

'There was absolutely a madness in it. It took two or three years to build this bridge. It was like this idea he had to get electricity to the house. He reclaimed land too, and then didn't know what to do with it.'

The bridge was a failure. The metal cylinders McColgan bought as a conduit for the stream lie there still, rusting in the water. The concrete pipe under the lane is dry, and the stream courses under the road as before. Among the browns and greys of the mountain side, there is a little green place with rushes and short grass beside the stream. 'I remember crouching down here, watching, waiting to be roared at to come and do something,' said Sophia. She picked a rush. 'We used to peel the green bark off these.' She walked along the lane, remembering. 'Imagine, a little child made to walk along here day after day, winter and summer, knowing what was ahead of her,' she said. 'Sometimes it would be pitch dark and raining when I would be brought here. It is just appalling what he did to us.'

A massive grey boulder lies at the last corner before the house. The house is small and low and well on the way to being a ruin. Below it, where the lane ends, there is a large modern structure made of concrete blocks cemented together. The walls are about four feet high, and the structure is about twelve feet deep. 'That's the cattle crush Michelle had to make,' said Sophia. 'She built all those walls with her bare hands.' Sophia walked ahead, picking out an overgrown narrow path up to the house. 'Look! There are footsteps. Someone has been up here,' she said. 'My father was always looking out for footsteps to see had anyone been prowling about.' She walked past the side of the house to the back, where a grove of hazel bushes and whitethorn stand. 'He raped me here among those trees. He was wearing his red overalls and they were covered in oil. It was one of the last rapes,' she said in a quiet voice. 'I'm just after remembering.'

She pointed out the place where McColgan blasted away a fragment of the mountain behind the house, hiring a rock breaker and transporting it up at great expense, and to no apparently useful end. 'He made enquiries about getting dynamite up here to do the job,' she said. 'I think he even went to the Gardaí to ask. You can imagine what that would have been like. He was supposed to be going to harness this wonderful natural stream down the side of the house to generate electricity. Nothing came of that either.'

Sophia walked through long grass to the broken-down stone walls of an ancient shed, where he'd left the little cow to die after she had fallen off a cliff. At the front of the house, she spotted a white motorbike helmet full of slimy green water. The helmet was cracked. 'That was his helmet,' she said. 'I'm surprised to see that there. He cracked it one time he had an accident. Not a serious one, unfortunately.'

Tangles of rope and wire and bits of broken things cut up through the grass. The earth has been scarred by McColgan, just as he scarred the skin of his children and his wife. Sophia climbed onto a window-sill and hoisted herself up to look in the tiny window upstairs to the left of the front door. 'That's the room,' she said. 'The chest is still in there.'

Walking away from this shell full of horrors, Sophia remembered the sheer physical labour that used to be involved in attempting to realise her father's grandiose ideas. 'He put tremendous effort into thinking up these things, but in the end it would be ourselves who did the work while he commanded the operation. He'd bring big heavy machines up here and they'd get stuck in the bog. We would have to use chains and planks and stones to try and get him out. He'd call over people who came up the mountain on a tractor to collect turf, and he'd get them to help too. Once he hired a Himac digger and he sank it to its cab in the bog. There it was, £15,000 worth of machinery sinking into the bog. It took days to dig it out.' When things did not work out, McColgan would line the children up and they would bow their heads as he berated them. It must have looked like those paintings of the labourers stopping to say the 'Angelus'. 'We were fear stricken,' said Sophia.

After we had come down the mountain, Sophia decided we should call on a man who used to live in the area. The man recognised Sophia instantly and greeted her. Sophia explained that we were working on a book about her life, and asked the man if he would like to contribute some of his memories in it. 'Arra, Sophie, he was good to me. He never did me any harm,' the man said. 'I wouldn't want to say anything against the man.' 'What good did he do you?' Sophia asked. She does not like to be called

Sophie, her father's name for her. 'Well, he did the odd favour for me,' said the man. 'What do you think about what he did to us, his children?' Sophia said. 'Well, that was desperate,' he said. 'According to what was in the papers, anyway.'

Sophia asked the man if he remembered the work the children had to do. 'Sure what harm was in that?' he replied. 'I remember poor Michelle right enough; she used to be perished lifting the blocks. I remember he used to be shouting at you, but I thought he was only messing. Do you remember, Sophie, you used to be up on the green place among the rushes reading your books?'

Sophia did not remember that. She was polite to the old man, but deeply shocked by his attitude. 'It's almost as if he doesn't really believe it happened,' she said. 'I sometimes feel that there are people who want me to stay in the world of silence. God knows, they are nice, decent people who probably never hurt a fly. But what sort of ignorance are we buried in? That is the kind of wall I've been coming across all my life, not just in this form, but in the educated sense as well. When you come to the educated person you are talking to a wall again, but this time the wall has defences.'

The plan Sophia conceived when she was thirteen — to use her education to save the family from her father — was never going to be an easy one to implement. She was a diligent student, but she did not learn quickly. She would need time to study, and her father did not give her time. 'I was just as military about my study as my father was about his abuse,' she said. 'From 1983 on, any time I had, even with him, I would study.' The little girl on a few minutes' break from building the rock bridge would sit on the green place and get out her books.

A neighbour from the foot of the mountain said that local farmers used to wonder what kept McColgan so late on the mountain at night. 'He would sometimes call in to my house after midnight, and he would chat away as if it was the middle of the day. Then when he'd go to leave, you'd realise that one of the family had been sitting outside the whole time on the bike, and it maybe raining or freezing,' said the man.

'We used to say among ourselves that it wasn't right. He made the family work so hard. I remember seeing Patsy with a roll of barbed wire under one arm and a child under the other. At the time I thought it was a terrible thing to see a woman treat a child that way, but now I know it was that she had to do it. I always remarked too how quick the McColgan children were to do what he said, no matter how unreasonable or hard it was. I know now it was fear, pure fear. We used to wonder, how were the children meant to get up for school in the morning.'

Until she developed the ability to leave her body, Sophia did not do well at school. She failed a lot of her exams in first year at the convent, but gradually picked up through the sheer force of her determination to succeed. 'I was fighting for my life, really,' she said. It would be nine or ten o'clock, sometimes later, when her father had finished with her on the mountain at night. 'He would be quite calm as we walked back to the bike,' she said. 'He would say that I was his, and that what he was doing to me was the most natural thing in the world. He used to give out about the Church's teaching about contraception. He said it was very necessary. He said everyone had the right to do this and that even after I was married, he would still do the same to me.'

The mountain lane was treacherous in the dark and McColgan drove recklessly. None the less, behind him, Sophia would already be working. 'I would be going over what I had done in class that day, trying to memorise it,' she said. Back at Cloonacurra, she would eat, if there was food, go hungry if there was not. By midnight, she was in her little room. 'There was no heat, so in the winter time I would put on old cardigans Granny had given me, and tights and socks and jeans. I used to be like an Eskimo. I had a hot water bottle too. In later years, my mother managed to get me an old oil heater. I would get my written homework out of the way first, and then I would study. I studied till three in the morning, and then I slept till seven.'

That was if her father left her in peace to sleep. One night, she was woken up to find him in the room with a camera. 'He had this polaroid camera he had borrowed. He took a horrible picture of me, forcibly. The next day, he cut it all up into pieces and he showed it to the children. He gave a tiny little piece to Michelle and he said, "That's Sophie." He was laughing,' she said. 'He was a pornographer.'

After a row in the house on Circular Road, McColgan refused to allow Sophia to go there any more after school. After that, she had to wait outside the convent for her father, or walk to the cathedral and wait for him there. 'I used to sit at the back of the cathedral,' she said. 'There would be very few people about. The cleaning women might be there, and there would be a few people around who weren't really the full shilling. I used to be half-afraid of some of the characters that would be lurking about. I'd be there for about two hours. It was very cold and gloomy. There used to be a few women about who would be feverish in their prayers. One day I'd been there since lunchtime, because it was a half-day at school. There was an old man there who often used to see me and he must have thought I was very devoted altogether. He came up to me and he said, "One day you will be a nun."'

The cathedral's grey bulk, faced across the road by the bishop's palace, stands on a road lined with several of the town's other great grey institutions, one of them Nazareth House, where Sophia was to have been sent in 1979 before the decision was taken that she would be better off back in her father's house.

Among the black limestone pillars, in the dim, stained-glass light, Sophia sat. Overlooked by statues of the Blessed Virgin and Christ on the cross, and surrounded by the murmur and chant of other people's prayers, she sat silently in the great vaulted chamber of God's house, and waited for her father.

'I would be constantly looking over my shoulder, waiting for him to appear,' she said. 'Every time the door opened, I'd be stretching around to see was it him. I remember one time the door opening and I saw him standing there, framed against the light, and he was in a bad mood. You'd always be wondering what sort of a temper he would be in. He stood there and he roared out of him, "Come on to fuck out of there. I haven't all day to be waiting around for you." The whole place echoed with the words he was saying. I'd been there for hours. I was hungry and cold and I had still to face the journey to the mountain and this thing I dreaded every day of my life.'

It wasn't just in the cathedral that Sophia felt anxious about other strange men. She would often be left on her own in the house at Cloonacurra, or in charge of the little ones in the family. She would be under orders that if anyone came about the place she was to tell them that this was private property and that trespassers would be prosecuted. 'I remember one night a stranger came and he wouldn't go away. He was prowling around the house and the sheds at the back. I was trying to study for an exam the next day, and I was scared. I did badly in the exam.'

Sophia's maternal grandparents are kindly people, and Michael had the habit of inviting people into their house in the village for tea. 'My father used to take these notions to try and outdo Grandad, and he would invite people into our house,' said Sophia. 'But they would always be outrageous people, people you wouldn't want to have about the place, people who would try to do things to you, like

107

kiss you.' McColgan humiliated his daughter about her developing body, forcing her to walk around the house in her pants, even when strangers were there. 'He was always embarrassing us. He did the weirdest things,' said Sophia, 'like the time he went out on the road in the nip and tried to hitch a lift. We were all hiding in the house, mortified. He thought he was great.'

'Sometimes, in the later years, we used to be able to laugh and see him as a complete fool. One time he was at the cattle mart with Michelle. He didn't understand at all the way the mart works and how the dealing is done. The farmers make deals by just the way they look at the auctioneer, or they'd wink or tip their hats or something. He kept on scratching his chin, wondering, or wiping his forehead, stressed about which sheep to buy. In the end, he bought a whole lot of sheep without realising it. The auctioneer was in a frenzy when he realised this man hadn't a clue. He was full sure my father had bought the lot, and it nearly came to blows. He took none of them. My sister came back and told us the story. It was so funny. At times you'd die laughing, he was so ridiculous. But at the same time, as soon as you saw him coming, you fell into your place and stayed in it. It was like a total withdrawal — hide, he's back.'

There was some small comfort in this, the sharing of occasional, hidden laughter. But it was impossible to go beyond it, to communicate about the brutality which had marooned each family member in their own private hell. 'He was constantly threatening me that if I opened my mouth he would kill me or some other member of the family,' said Sophia. 'Not only that, but if I tried to get in contact with Michelle to make an ally, he would always be one step ahead of me. One time I said something to Michelle, something mild like, "He is not being very nice to me." And I left it like that for a bit, and then I asked her, casually, "Can you keep a secret?" I was just testing to see would she tell or could I get her confidence first. Unfortunately, she told him straight away, he had her so terrorised into telling everything. If she didn't tell and he found out during interrogation, she'd get bad abuse.'

'She told him and he came back at me and nearly killed me with his hands and feet, hitting me and kicking me. He liked to stick his fingers under my chin,' she said, demonstrating the action. 'In here, under where my tongue is. He loved to pressurise it. He made sure I wasn't going to try that again. He was always ahead of me, every time I tried to do anything. He'd figure it out and put a stop to it. If I could only have got Michelle to trust me, we could have put our heads together and maybe found a way out together. But he was always there, interrogating. His mood swings were incredible. One minute he was quiet and the next thing there was this storm of false allegations, and setting one person up against another over nothing. Michelle was very artistic. In the later years she did some amazing paintings. They would be raging with temper. His violence was in those pictures. He found them and confiscated them.'

'We were prisoners in a tower with no door. The care workers, so-called, knew we were in prison, but they didn't seem to care. They looked and then they looked away again. I was trying to make a door to let other people see in, and to let us out, but sometimes I felt like the Lady of Shallot. She was locked up in a tower and she could not even look out. She used to weave a tapestry all day, and she watched the world in a mirror. In the end, she sees the handsome knight in the mirror and she is tempted and she turns and looks. She leaves the tower then and gets in a boat and floats down the river to Camelot. She is beautiful, but she dies.'

Sophia loved the Tennyson poem. She felt that perhaps the only escape for her would be death too.

'She loosed the chain, and down she lay;
The broad stream bore her far away,
The Lady of Shalott.'

Other times she fantasised that her own Sir Lancelot would come riding down the Sligo to Galway road on his charger, stop at her wretched home in Cloonacurra, and take her away to happiness. 'There was one lad in the village who liked me a lot. I had heard a rumour to that effect anyway. Sometimes when my father was out, I used to sneak out on the bike and go up to the shop in the village to get a few messages for my mother. I might buy a few cakes to bring home. It would be like this big adventure, with the risk that he would catch you leaving or arriving back. This day, anyway, I put on some make-up,' she said, with a great laugh. 'I headed up the village and sure enough this lad must have liked me because he stood like a statue by the shed outside the school. I thought, maybe he'll be brave and approach me. There was no way I could approach him. I said to myself, he looks strong and quiet and nice. Maybe he'll come and save me and make me feel happy and good about life.'

In 1987, Sophia's great-grandmother, Great-Granny Mullen, died after a long illness. McColgan forbade his family to attend the removal, though after a long argument he let them go to the funeral. 'He hated her because she believed in freedom,' said Sophia. 'At the funeral, I just felt so hurt. I loved her so much, but because of my father, our relationship was completely destroyed. I couldn't talk to her. I was afraid to tell her how unhappy I was and what was really going on. She was a great woman, very strong and proud. I learned after she died that, when I was small, she'd written a letter to Grandad. She had realised early on with my father that he was cruel. I think she knew it was more than physical. She felt he should be watched. My grandparents already felt the same, but there was nothing they could do. If Granny even said something trivial about our health or well-being, my father would beat us over it. I think if Great-Granny Mullen had known the half of what he was doing, she'd have shot him, and I believe she was a good shot. A man spoke at her funeral about what she had done for the struggle for Irish freedom. She went down with a tricolour. I feel I get my steel from her. After she died, there was a huge gap.'

McColgan sneered at Sophia's efforts at school.

When I got my Junior Cert results when I was fifteen, he was disgusted. He said they were useless. Somebody down the road had got brilliant results, all A's and B's. He went on and on about the child who had got these results and that mine were a disgrace, even though I got six honours and I was going through hell on earth. Granny Sally was delighted with me and Grandad must have given me half a block of ice-cream in a wafer. My father would not let me stay to eat it though, so I had to eat it on the motorbike.

I had come to secondary school at a disadvantage anyway, as the girls who had been to town schools were better prepared. At my national school in the country, we hadn't done French, whereas the other girls had already made a good start with it. I did my best to catch up, but it wasn't good enough. I did manage to get, after tremendous hard work, six honours in the Junior Cert, but I needed seven. I passed French but I needed to do it as an honours subject for my Leaving Cert.

Sophia was far too driven to be discouraged.

I fought with teachers and the principal to be allowed to do French for the Leaving. I remember one of the teachers said something to me in French about Bob Geldof and 'Live Aid' and I didn't have a clue. She said, 'Can you tell me what that was about?' and I couldn't, but I still insisted and they were very, very annoyed at me. They said, 'No way, you are just not good enough at French. You have to have an honour in the Junior Cert before you can do the Leaving Cert. I got an awful telling off. But I did honours, despite what they said.

I did know about 'Live Aid', because it was in the summer time and I think we had a TV then. I thought Bob Geldof was great. He was shouting for the rights of children and he was very emotional and dedicated to his cause. I know he had a lot of money but he turned the world to look at those poor starving children in Ethiopia. While it was happening, though, I was undergoing a different kind of tyranny. My father claimed he thought Bob Geldof was great too, but it was only to make him look good in the eyes of other people.

For the first year of the Leaving Certificate course, her fifth year at the Ursuline, Sophia failed every single French exam, Christmas, Easter and summer. 'It was only at Christmas in sixth year that I passed anything, and that was incredible — I got an honour. It was because my Granny Sally had given me some money secretly to get grinds. If he'd known I had the money, he'd have taken it. He always took any money we got. The way he looked at it, he owned us so he owned our money too. I told him I had to go to extra classes because we were doing some French drama. He didn't know I was paying. Later on he copped on that

I was doing grinds, but funnily enough he went along with it, fortunately for me. I was never sure what his attitude to my studies was. Sometimes he'd say education was important and he'd go to great lengths to get me to school, even through the snow. He pretended he was a real Dad who cared. Towards the end of my time at the Ursuline he actually paid for some grinds for me. He never thought I'd succeed anyway.'

Astonishingly, Sophia not only managed to keep up with her schoolwork, she also took on additional work, studying home economics as an extra subject in her own time. Part of the curriculum was biology, which she loved, and which also helped her to develop a good attitude to her body as a foil to the distorted view her father was giving her. 'Part of it was psychology, how to deal with grief and a whole lot of things. I was striving to learn about my situation while using my education as the best way to figure a way out of it.'

She sat her Leaving Certificate exams in 1988. Summer on the mountain followed. Her father had taken to bringing the family to the mountain house and making them stay there. 'He was always strangling me,' said Sophia. 'I remember my mother and Michelle coming to the house and I was passing out. He told my mother to watch me, because I kept losing consciousness. Something awful was after happening to me, but I do not remember what it was. At the cottage, too, he would fix his hands around my throat. One time I was standing at the cooker and I fell asleep and suddenly he was shaking me. It took me a few minutes to realise that I was Sophia McColgan and I lived in this family and he was my father and I had brothers and sisters. I felt totally disorientated. It took me about an hour to realise that he had done it.'

'There is a lot from those years that I do not remember. My memory has blocked it out. And then, I didn't know the half of what he was doing because I wasn't there. I had left my body. In counselling I am remembering and, this time, I feel the pain I avoided at the time. The pain is extraordinary. Doing these interviews for the book is bringing back a lot of deeply buried memories too. In the High Court I remembered a lot, but already, just a few months later, I know that if I took the stand I could talk for weeks. I could probably remember every day of my life, and every day has its violence. During those years when I was studying, I just had that thin thread that I was holding on to for my survival. I *had* to get my degree.'

As she grew older, Sophia began to fight her father. 'I was fighting with great mental strength against him,' she said. 'Sometimes I tried physically to stop him too. He would twist my arms and squeeze my hands until my fingers nearly broke. He liked to stick needles into me as well. He'd be picking at his teeth with a needle and then he'd stick it into you and when you screamed he laughed. I was fighting him and struggling, but he always overpowered me. He was a big man and I was a small girl. I realised I was trapped.'

The Leaving Cert results were a blow. Sophia failed to get the four honours she needed to go to college. 'I was devastated,' she said. 'I got two honours, but I needed four to get a scholarship. I thought, "I won't get to college with these results. He will win."'

However, it was a setback, not a defeat. Sophia rallied, and persuaded her father to let her repeat her final year. His violence at home continued unabated, though he was not sexually abusing Sophia to the same extent as before. Unknown to her, he had by this stage turned the force of his sexual attentions onto Michelle. One day, during 1989, in that final year at school, Sophia was studying in her bedroom when her father came in. 'He made some perverted demand of me and I tried to refuse. I said, "No". I defied him and told him that what he was doing was wrong. He put me into a situation in which I was screaming with pain. He said, "Say it is right." I said, "It is right."'

McColgan then dragged his eighteen-year-old daughter by her hair out into the living room so that the rest of the family could learn by her example. He pulled her to the front door and smashed her head through one of its glass panels. The other children and their mother watched in horror. 'All I remember is feeling dizzy and the glass on the floor,' said Sophia. 'I got up. Everything was going around in the room. Things were moving. The chairs. The people were talking. He was talking. His head was moving over and back. It was the way my head was spinning. After that, I didn't dare try anything like that again. I knew what was coming to me.'

While Sophia could be forced to agree, she was privately pushing herself to her outermost limits in the struggle to defeat her father. 'He could make me say yes, but in my own mind, I was saying, "That's what you think, but I think differently."' In the Leaving Cert exams of 1989, Sophia got five honours. 'I was just pure determined.'

'The day of our graduation, the nuns put out the long tables. After the graduation mass with the parents, we had tea. All the other girls were going out that night, everyone except me. One girl felt sorry for me, Nicola. I think she knew by the way I said "No" when she asked was I coming to the disco, that it wasn't my own choice, though I was afraid to say it. I felt so left out of everything because of the way my life was. Nicola plucked up her courage to ask her mother to ask my father. It turned out this woman had known my father when they were at school, so she went and asked him would it be all right if I went to the disco and stayed over at their house. He was very reluctant, but in the end he was embarrassed into agreeing.'

This was wonderful. Sophia remembers going to Nicola's house at Strandhill, full of excitement. She took off her school uniform for the last time. 'I remember dressing up in clothes belonging to Nicola, a green shirt and pink trousers. We went to the pictures in Sligo first, and saw "Three Men and a Baby". I thought it was brilliant. I loved it. Afterwards we went to the disco at the Great Southern Hotel. It was a girls' night out. I think we got in free.' When she came out of the disco, he was waiting for her on the Honda 50. 'He'd promised I could stay at Nicola's, but he brought me home.'

Worse was to follow. The next day was the graduation dinner in the Sligo Park Hotel.

He wasn't going to let me go, and then he decided I would go. All the other girls had been talking for months about what dress they would be wearing — it would be this style or that style, and so and so would be making it for them, or it would be from such and such a boutique. My father brought me to this crummy old shop in Ballymote, and he made me get this dress which was meant for a sixty-year old. It was blue with black diamond shapes. It was horrid to say the least and I felt so awful in it. He made me wear my hair all up in a bun on top of my head.

He thought he was teaching me a lesson, by making everyone laugh at me. It was like the way someone might give a child a cigarette to make them sick, so that they won't ever smoke again. He had already told me about how when he was younger he had brought a girl to the Ursuline graduation dinner himself. He said he had painted his car and when they arrived, the nuns came out to meet them and the girl stepped out of the car only to find her dress was covered in paint. He said he thought this was hilarious. Anyway, we arrived at the hotel. One of the teachers met us in the lobby. She was in her stylish little black French number, and there I was, bright red and in this horrible outfit. My father had brought my mother too, and she was there stiff beside him.

The teacher said, 'Mr McColgan, you'll sit over on the far side with the other parents.' But he wasn't having that. He was insisting that he would sit with me. He created a huge row over it. I remember Pat Kenny was in the lobby that night, in a shiny suit and dickie bow. The other girls were going, 'Oh look, there's Pat Kenny!' One of the other girls was crazy about him and she had told me she had sent him a photo of herself. He was very kind and sent her one of himself back. Anyway, he was there at some other function.

Eventually the teacher said my father would be thrown out, so he went to sit with the parents. I was the only girl at the long table with no partner opposite me. There was a disco afterwards. All the other parents left, but he stayed and he kept my mother there too. He sat and watched me. All the lads and girls were shifting each other in front of him. It was all so ridiculous. Gerry was over from England at that time and he had a car so he brought me home. My father brought my mother home on the motorbike. He thought he had taught me a lesson.

Sophia had applied to the Dublin Institute of Technology in Bolton Street to do applied science, and now had the points to go there. 'I wanted to go,' she said. 'I didn't have much interest in the course, but I wanted to get away from my father. I thought I'd get the chance to socialise and see what normal life was like, even though it would be in at the deep end. I thought I could find my bearings, and what better place than in the capital. I wanted to develop, and I knew I could learn a lot.'

The other course for which she was accepted was environmental science and technology at Sligo's Regional Technical College (RTC). 'I felt that if I stayed at home I could stop the others from getting the abuse which I was getting,' she said. 'It was like a game of chess between me and my father. It took a long time to make each move, because if I made a mistake, someone could get killed. I'd seen my father lose his temper and it wasn't a pretty sight. The blood, the tears, people passing out. It was better to make no move at all than to make a wrong one.' Sophia realised besides that she could not afford to go to Dublin. 'I loved the course on offer in Sligo and I knew in my heart I had no choice.'

9

'I SAW THIS MORNING SOPHIA SMILING'

❧❦❧

Sophia the student was terrified of everybody and everything in this new, informal environment of sociable, easy-going young people. 'I was scared of everything that moved,' she said, 'because I didn't know how the real world worked. I didn't know how to fit in.' Her father continued to use his old tactics to embarrass her in front of her peers. He would make sure she was late for college in the morning, driving her noisily to the door on the motorbike, and he would turn up during the day in his filthy overalls and wellingtons demanding to see her. 'He used to roar and shout at me and throw down his motorbike helmet.'

'Those were to be the last two years I lived at home, and they were really a battle between us. He knew I was onto something. He was determined to wreck it for me. I was just as determined that I would get him put away. The fight was in my head. He'd say one thing to me, and I'd say "Yes," but what I'd think was, "You are badly mistaken." I wasn't dealing with a normal run-of-the-mill person. I was dealing with someone well used to plotting. He plotted his abuse of each and every one of us. I sort of knew his mind, but he could still catch me. You'd think he wouldn't know what you were thinking, but he did.'

Timid and silent, Sophia at first did her best to be inconspicuous at the college. Arriving late was painful. 'I remember one morning I knocked on the door of the classroom, but I must have knocked very, very weakly,' she said. 'The lecturer looked up when he saw me coming in and he said, "What's the name of that famous shrine up the road?" It didn't dawn on me what he was talking about. I just stood there, saying nothing. Then someone else shouted out, "Knock". Everyone laughed, but I couldn't laugh. I was under so much pressure. I'm sure people thought I was extremely odd. I feared for my sanity.'

Gradually, she began to find that she liked her fellow students, and that they were not threatening to her. 'I tried to be nice to people without divulging any information about myself,' she said. 'After a while, I realised that it was fine. The people were very nice. I could get by. I didn't have to tell people what I was really about to get by from day to day.' She relaxed into her old skill of pretending to be just like everyone else. The devastation within her she kept firmly at bay.

When she was a schoolgirl, Sophia had been so horrified by her sexual experiences at the hands of her father that she felt no inclination to explore her own sexuality. 'I never wanted a "first kiss" from a boy,' she said. Now, aged nineteen, she realised she was attracted to boys. 'At first I was terrified of them. My father had made me that way. He was constantly warning me that men were all only out to rape you. I am so grateful that, having a loving and kind grandfather, I knew that not all men were like my father. At college I began to realise I liked fellows big time.'

However, liking was one thing — being able to do anything about it was another. Once, during one of her father's rants in front of the college, he threw down his helmet and it landed at the feet of a boy to whom Sophia was attracted. 'I nearly died. I had asked my father if I could go to the cinema. He said "No" and threw a scene. I realised I was trapped. Socialising was out. I couldn't afford to make a wrong move, so it had to be sacrificed. I longed to have friends, people who liked me for myself and who realised that if I was weird, it was for a reason. But it wasn't to be. I just had to concentrate on getting the degree.'

Once during this time, an aunt brought Sophia and Michelle to the forest park at Boyle, County Roscommon, a short drive away from Cloonacurra. 'We had a lovely day,' said Sophia. 'We walked in the woods and looked at the trees and then we went into a hotel for tea. The young fellow who served the tea let the pot slip and it scalded my foot. The manager was very apologetic and I was brought to a doctor in Boyle. When I got home, I was trying to hide it from my father because I knew he'd raise a huge fuss over it. But I couldn't wear anything over the wound, so he did notice it and of course he insisted on suing. I felt so sorry for the young fellow. I didn't want to get him into trouble. After all, what he did was an accident, and here was my father, who was getting away with incredible violence and abuse, complaining.'

One of Sophia's lecturers remembers her as 'a very gentle person'. The lecturer said that when she learned, when Sophia and her family gave up their anonymity in 1997, what Sophia's true story was, she found it almost impossible to imagine that the quiet, polite young person she knew had experienced so much brutality. 'There was no roughness in her. You'd expect a person who had had that kind of life to have a roughness to them. She was a good student. She was never part of a gang. She was like the Blessed Virgin in a play, lovely, almost otherworldly.'

One night, Sophia did try to persuade her father to allow her to go to a party in Cartron Bay, a housing estate on the edge of

Sligo's harbour. It is the town's flatland. He refused. She pleaded. He twisted her arm and slapped her about until she cried out and said she didn't want to go.

'I was an extremely lonely, lonely person,' she said. 'I used to read poetry. At the Ursuline a lot of the other girls used to laugh at poetry and they hated having to study it. I loved it. I love Donne, and the Romantics, Wordsworth and Shelley. I read Kavanagh a lot too. I like Donne because he talks about how our body only dresses the soul. I was out of my body for a lot of my life. I didn't care about my body. I was so hurt I couldn't feel my pain. Donne reflected a lot of my misery. Funerals feature a lot in his poems.

'I love Shelley's poem about dying. He drowned not long after he wrote it. In the poem, he is sitting on the beach looking at the beautiful sea and he imagines what it would be like to have someone else there to share it with. But he is alone. He imagines himself slipping away . . .'

> 'Alas! I have nor hope nor health,
>   Nor peace within nor calm around,
> Nor that content surpassing wealth
>   The sage in meditation found,
> And walked with inward glory crowned —
>   Nor fame, nor power, nor love, nor leisure.
> Others I see whom these surround —
>   Smiling they live, and call life pleasure;—
> To me that cup has been dealt in another measure.
>
> Yet now despair itself is mild,
>   Even as the winds and waters are;
> I could lie down like a tired child,
>   And weep away the life of care

Which I have borne and yet must bear,
  Till death like sleep might steal on me,
And I might feel in the warm air
  My cheek grow cold, and hear the sea
Breathe o'er my dying brain its last monotony.'

(from 'Stanzas. Written in dejection, near Naples', by Percy Bysshe Shelley)

'At times my need to die was very great,' said Sophia. 'It seemed a nice thing to do. It was like a hope, a fantasy, like the man on the horse who would come to save me.'

At home, the abuse went on. 'He had mellowed a bit towards me in terms of the hard, physical violence, and the sexual violence, but he would make me sit on his knee and say all kinds of disgusting things. The mental abuse continued as bad as ever, the endless interrogations and threats. I knew I couldn't leave home, or he would kill me or kill someone else. We still had to wait on him hand and foot, change his socks, get his boots, do the work. He had us as slaves.'

Sally remembers that during this time, Joe McColgan would bring Patsy and the family to her house for Sunday dinner, but would leave early with Michelle, who would obviously not want to go with him. He had also taken to guarding Michelle particularly closely, rarely letting her out of his sight. She had become silent and withdrawn.

In 1991, all changed for Sophia, when suddenly, at the age of twenty-one, she was thrown out of the prison that was her home. 'It was in the middle of the night,' she said. 'I was asleep in bed when he came into the room and dragged me out. He accused me of refusing to lend my Walkman to Michelle. It was completely mad. He got extremely angry. He gave me a fierce beating. Then he told me to get out of his house; he'd had enough of me. He said all kinds of ridiculous things. I think he said I was no child of his, and that I should have been a boy. He was ranting and raving. He said, "You can get out now and take the road — there's the gate." I remember being quite brave then. I said I wasn't leaving without my college folder. I had an exam two weeks later and my notes were all there. I took the folder and I said something to him. I think I said, "Wait till you see. One of these days you'll regret the way you've treated me." It was a risky thing to say, but he had beaten me so badly I reckoned maybe his energy was spent.'

However, once out on the dark road, wearing nothing but her nightdress and clutching the precious folder, Sophia's bravery flew to the winds and the terror returned. In her bare feet, she ran into the night. Her only refuge was with her Granny at Ballinacarrow, a mile and a half away. A few cars passed her, a mysterious barefoot young woman in a nightdress, running along a country road in the middle of the night. Nobody stopped. Suddenly, she thought she heard her father's motorbike revving up. Fearing what would happen if he caught her, she dived off the road and down the steep ditch to the field by the river. The river was in flood, and she almost slipped into its fast brown waters as she scrambled under the old stone bridge below the road.

> 'She loosed the chain, and down she lay;
> The broad stream bore her far away,
> The Lady of Shalott.'

Once again, death was tempting. But her fierce will not to be destroyed by her father rallied, and she struggled on. She would never live in her father's house again.

Sally remembers that night. 'We were asleep in bed. It must have been about four in the morning and next thing we heard a tap tap on the window and Sophia's voice. She said, "Granny, it's Sophia that's in it. Let me in. He's after me." She was terrorised. She was shaking from head to foot with fear, and perished,' Sally said. Sally filled hot water bottles, got Sophia a dry nightdress, wrapped her up and put her in a bed with an electric blanket. 'She kept on saying, "He'll get in. He'll get me here."' Sophia also told her Granny that her father had been 'treating me like a wife'. Sally said she took this to mean that he expected her to do all the work about the house. 'She was hysterical with fear,' she said. Eventually, Sophia slept.

She was feverish and ill for weeks, Sally recalls. 'She would waken up in the night roaring and crying. She would be screaming, "He's coming in the door. He's going to kill me!"' said Sally. 'I would get up and tell her she was all right. I told her if he came in my door he wouldn't go out again. But she was terrorised.'

McColgan was meanwhile sounding forth on child psychology. A neighbour from the mountain land at Killerry remembers him calling to his house around this time. 'I asked one of my own children to do something for me and she said she hadn't time or something,' said the neighbour, a farmer who had often helped McColgan out. 'So he said, "You wouldn't know how to raise children nowadays. I have a daughter at home, she's twenty-one, and the other day I asked her to make a cup of tea for me. She said she would not and she ran out of the house and into a drain."'

❧❀❧

Sophia stayed with her grandparents for the remainder of her college years. Her father would come to the house and threaten her still, telling her that he would take a knife to her if she told on him. One day, he pursued her around her grandmother's kitchen, trying to get at her to beat her. More than once, her grandfather, Michael, who had been a boxer in his youth in London, took a swing at McColgan to get him out of the house.

Learning did not come easily to Sophia. She believes she had to work three times as hard as a person from a normal background, just to keep up. 'I studied morning, noon and night, weekends, holidays, all the time. I studied even when there were no exams coming up. I researched and went into book after book looking for new knowledge. I will never work as hard again as I worked for that degree. My father was the driving force behind me. He might as well have been behind me with a knife. I didn't let anyone know I was working so hard because they would have thought I was a total fruitcake.'

Sophia said she needed a lot of reassurance. 'I was constantly going to the head of the course wanting to know was I doing all right. He said I was doing fine.' She became possessed of a new imperative — a simple degree would not do. She was going for honours. 'I felt that would improve my credibility,' she said.

Two weeks after her twenty-first birthday, a month after he had thrown her out of the house, her father turned up at the college. 'I was in the canteen talking to another girl and suddenly I saw him. The girl said to me, "Sophia, what's wrong? You're as white as a ghost." He had brought my mother and she was there beside him, ashen-faced as usual. He had on his suit and he had a huge bunch of flowers in his hands. He had presents of gold jewellery, a ring and a bracelet engraved with "To Sophie, love from Daddy and Mammy and the kids". I said I didn't want them. I said, "Why did you beat us?" He said he was sorry, he hadn't meant it. He asked me to come home. He was still pushing these presents at me.

I said I didn't want them. My mother pleaded with me to take them. "Take them, Sophie, please take them," she said. I knew she'd get beaten up if I didn't, so I took them. I gave the flowers to Grandad for the chapel and I never wore the jewellery.'

Away from the hated presence of her father, Sophia began to test the waters of normal life. Before she was thrown out of home, one of McColgan's brothers had talked him into letting Sophia go to America to work during the summer of her second year at college. McColgan allowed her to make all the arrangements, then said she couldn't go. Once she was no longer in her father's house, she realised that she could go after all. 'I was twenty-one, but I was really green when I went to the States. I hadn't a clue. My uncle had told me that when I arrived in the airport in New York, I was to look as if I knew what I was doing and where I was going, because there would be people there watching out for someone who looked like they had landed on Mars.'

My uncle met me and he brought me in a Cadillac up to Atlantic City. I worked as a waitress, a barmaid, a receptionist and even a chambermaid. I worked all day, every day, from early morning until late at night. I discovered in America that even if you were the dumbest person with no skills whatsoever, people still think you are great. It is a very positive society. I loved it. I know a lot of people back home would think it was over the top, ridiculous and materialistic. But it suited me fine. I'd never seen anything nice in my life and here was all this glitzy world around me.

It gave me confidence about myself. I told the manager of a restaurant that I could waitress when really I had never waitressed in my life, and a few hours later, there I was, a waitress. There was a big fellow in the kitchen, a black fellow called Herman. He used to roar out at me in his American accent, 'Sophia, is it baked potato, mashed potato or French fries?' I was always forgetting to put that on the docket. I was well liked in America. I had an ability to chat to people. I made a huge effort to make it work.

I was there for a couple of months. It toughened me up in a good way. It wised me up. To my surprise, I was quite capable. I used to go down to the First Fidelity Bank and I watched my savings grow. I took two trips, one to Baltimore and one to Washington. I didn't want to leave. I didn't have Ireland, silences, my father worrying the hell out of me. I temporarily forgot the terror.

While I was there, a grand-uncle came to visit me and he brought me gambling. Into the casino we went, Caesar's Palace, and he gave me a bucket of quarters. He pointed to the one-armed bandit and he said, 'You go over there and have some fun.' He took the time to come and see me. It was one of the first nice things that had ever happened to me in my entire life, that this man who hardly knew me had made that effort. He was Granny Sally's brother, Michael. When he died in 1997, they found out that he had all these medals from the Korean war that he had never talked about. He was a lovely man.

Sophia cried on the flight back to Ireland. Back home, the struggle to succeed and defeat her father resumed. She was full of guilt and anxiety. But at last, for the first time since she was five, she was being looked after. Sally coaxed her to eat, and gave her the love and nurturing she had been starved of for so long. The RTC was also a sympathetic environment. 'I began to realise that the other students liked me, even though they couldn't figure me out.

There were lots of people who wanted to know what made me tick. They were all so protective of me that I began to come out, slowly and very cautiously. I remember going with a girl into town and I bought a silky black see-through blouse. I also had a black clingy dress. One of the lecturers said I was like a caterpillar turning into a butterfly. I took a drink, for the first time, and then sometimes I'd even have enough drink to have a laugh and make a fool of myself.'

'I started to go out with a lad. He was a wonderful person, a lovely fellow. It was nice to meet a companion my own age. We went for walks. He taught me to swim. I had always been terrified of water because of my father trying to drown us. Swimming was brilliant. I began to be able to relax.' Once, she invited a fellow with whom she was friendly to tea at her Granny's. Sally went to some trouble, making a salad and setting the table nicely. She knew it was something for Sophia to be able to entertain a guest at home, especially a boy. They had just sat down to eat, when McColgan arrived. 'He came in sneering and he sat himself roughly down at the table,' said Sophia. 'He was filthy. He helped himself to food, and then he looked my friend up and down and made some disparaging remark. It was me he was getting at — he was letting me know that he didn't see this fellow as any threat to him.'

Sophia and her Granny took to going to Saturday evening mass in the village. McColgan always went to Sunday mass. However, one Saturday evening, not long after he had thrown her out, Sophia was horrified when her father walked into the chapel. 'I froze. He marched my mother in front of him up the aisle to the front. It was his way of warning me that if I tried anything, she would get hurt. My Granny whispered to me, "Don't worry, Sophia, if he comes near you I'll stick a knife in him."'

Sophia used to have to hitch-hike from Ballinacarrow into Sligo to the college and home again in the evening. She didn't like it, but her grant was not enough to allow her to travel by bus every day. 'I often wonder was that why the authorities didn't care about me — I was just a poor girl from a poor family. I was afraid, but I had developed this ability to chat. I remember once when I was only a small child, about four I think, my father was over from England and he had me in town at his parents'. He sent me home to Granny's in a car with a complete stranger. When we got to Ballinacarrow this man was saying to them all that I was a great little girl altogether, that I'd chatted the whole way. He said I had a great imagination and I could talk the hind legs off a duck. I was actually terrified. It was a case of keep talking . . . Other times, though, I'd go stone silent.'

Stone silent she remained about how she had been brutalised, and the terror which still stalked her. These were still terrible secrets which she did not dare expose. 'In a way, I was never really there,' said Sophia. 'Even when I had my college boyfriend, I felt that if I told him, I'd lose him. I never let anyone get too close. I felt really bad, really disgusting. I blamed myself for all that had happened to me. I felt that if I had never been born my father wouldn't have been a child abuser. I knew even then I wasn't thinking straight. I was sort of absent.'

Much of what had happened to her lay deeply buried in her mind, inaccessible even to herself. She knew the life she had lived, but she also knew that if she allowed her memories to ambush her, she would be overwhelmed and destroyed. Her college friends did not know the fierce Sophia McColgan who was fighting for her life against her brutal father. The Sophia that people met during those years was really the Sophia who came to call to her friend down the road from the mountain house. She was the Sophia that Sophia imagined.

Sophia's state of mind during the years immediately after she legally became an adult in 1988 was the subject of long days of argument during the High Court damages case. The NWHB and Dr Moran both claimed that Sophia was 'statute barred' from suing them. The Statute of Limitations states that a person suing for damages must do so within three years. In Sophia's case, she was alleging negligence on the part of medical professionals throughout her childhood, and the Board and the doctor said that, under the statute, she should have sued within three years of reaching the age of majority, that is, between 1988 and 1991. Sophia's Counsel claimed that because of the effects of sexual, physical and mental abuse, she was, during the period in question, 'of unsound mind' and therefore unable to contemplate a legal action.

'I saw this morning Sophia smiling,' observed John Rogers, Senior Counsel for the defence, suggesting that Sophia, whom he had noticed having a conversation with some of her lawyers in the great hall of the Four Courts in Dublin, seemed like a perfectly normal young woman. He asked Sophia why she had chosen not to tell anyone about the abuse she had suffered. 'I couldn't have done it any other way,' she said. 'I needed the strength that I had to complete my degree because if I had let it cascade on top of me, all that had happened to me, I would not have completed my degree and I would have failed that too. So I applied whatever energy I had to get my degree first before I made my statements to put my father in jail.'

Sabina Christensen, a Limerick-based psychologist who has worked extensively with survivors of child abuse, told the High Court that Sophia had been severely traumatised.

The greatest trauma to any individual occurs when the abuse happens over a long period of time, which was the case for Sophia; when the victim is closely related to the perpetrator, which again was the case for Sophia; when penetration has occurred, again in Sophia's case; and when it is accompanied by aggression.

Ms Christensen said that Sophia would have been debilitated by post-traumatic stress disorder. She described classic symptoms, including detachment from her feelings and social relationships, numbness towards trauma, flashbacks and intrusive memories and low self-esteem. She said that when she met Sophia in 1995, all these indicators were present. 'Not only did Sophia meet these criteria, but she met them in a very extreme way,' she said. Asked to rate Sophia's trauma on a scale of one to ten, Ms Christensen said that Sophia would be near to ten.

Sophia's symptoms were 'very classical and very typical', according to Ms Christensen. 'In a life where you have never got control, where you have always been out of control or where somebody has always controlled from the very, very minute detail of her functioning, you actually try desperately for a way to survive and to find some area of your life to control, to be in control, to feel somewhat normal and to get some sort of identity,' she said. Sophia had done this by investing all her energy in her academic studies. Ms Christensen said it was quite normal for a person who was unable to cope with parts of a life damaged by abuse, to be able to function exceptionally well in other parts.

Professor Ivor Browne, psychiatrist and psychotherapist, told the High Court that Sophia and her siblings had lived through 'the equivalent of years in a Nazi concentration camp', adding, 'No one can make normal, rational decisions in that sort of a situation.' He described Sophia's decision to use her education to find a way of tackling her father's abuse of the family as 'a survival operation taken desperately', rather than the rational decision it was described as by Counsel for the health professionals. Professor

Browne said that Sophia had created and lived in 'a frozen present', not really experiencing the things that had happened to her.

He defined as 'dissociation' Sophia's ability to leave her body during rapes on the mountain. 'Dissociation may also take the form of psychic numbing. A person simply is able to cut off the sensory stimuli that are happening during an abusive experience. It may also take the form of cutting off all the emotions that can accompany an abusive experience, so the person is aware of what is happening but is shielded or walled off from the psychological impact, the terror, for example.'

It was put to Professor Browne, by Mr Rogers, that his comparison of Sophia's sufferings with those of people in a Nazi concentration camp was 'going too far'. Mr Rogers said that in the camps millions of people were tortured and subjected to mass degradation. 'Isn't it the case that her father was a man who satisfied his own needs and wants through violence and sexual pleasure with his children?' he said. 'It is of a different order from torture.' Professor Browne insisted that he was not being histrionic. The children were tortured, he said, and they were also at risk of, and in terror of, death at the hands of their father. 'We have to regard this as a reign of terror on a daily basis.'

Counsel for Dr Moran, Patrick Hanratty, dismissed Professor Browne's description of 'a serious mental disability and incapacity' in Sophia during her early adulthood. 'The picture you are painting of this mental disability as a result of this emotional trauma is entirely at variance with the factual situation when you look at it coldly and clinically,' said Mr Hanratty. He said that in 1989, Sophia had 'got a grip on her life' and decided to do a degree. Mr Cooney interjected when Mr Hanratty referred to Sophia getting herself 'alternative accommodation' in 1991. 'If my friend believes being thrown out of your house, seeking refuge in your grandparents' house, is obtaining alternative accommodation, so be it,' he said.

It was Dr Suzanne Sgroi who put Sophia's situation into context in the starkest way in the High Court.

I think this case represents as severe a case of combined mental, physical and sexual abuse and exposure to domestic violence as I have seen in my career, with the exception of a few cases that had all of those elements in which people were killed.

Dr Sgroi runs a clinic devoted to cases of sexual abuse of children in Connecticut. She began to work in the field in 1972 when, as a medical doctor, she noted the prevalence of sexually transmitted diseases in children. She has written several books and numerous articles, and is regarded as one of the world's leading authorities on child sex abuse, its detection and treatment.

Dr Sgroi, along with Dr Alice Swann, the Belfast doctor who has been a pioneer in the field of understanding child abuse, had a consultation with Sophia in Dublin during the High Court case. Dr Sgroi said that Sophia's belief that her degree would save her and save her family had been an obsession.

She talked repeatedly, during the consultation, about her capacity in the pursuit of this to wall herself off, if you will, emotionally, from all of the danger and the violence and the unpredictability and the chaos of her father's home at that time in that first two years of college.

Asked by Mr Rogers whether this was a normal and appropriate response to her situation, Dr Sgroi was adamant. 'In my opinion she and the family were living with a dangerously disturbed individual who was threatening not only their physical safety but their very lives. The appropriate thing to do at that point would have been to preserve life by removing herself from that situation.' Dr Sgroi said that it was a 'thinking error' on Sophia's part that she could make herself safe and protect her family by getting a university degree.

Dr Sgroi said that Sophia had been able to increase her capacity to tolerate living in her father's house, where she was at risk of her life, 'by pushing away the fear and the terror and losing herself in study'. When Mr Rogers suggested that Sophia's decision to study for a degree and thereby make herself a more credible witness was 'sound', Dr Sgroi retorted, 'I don't think so, sir. She could have died.' She said it was a thinking error to believe 'that time will stop and a dangerous person who repeatedly threatens you and has demonstrated a willingness to use severe physical violence will somehow stay on hold until you have acquired a degree'.

Looking back further, to Sophia's early teenage years, Dr Sgroi identified another distortion in Sophia's thinking. She said Sophia had recognised that while Gerry was in the home, he was the 'lightning rod' for the abuse — in other words, its primary recipient. After he left, Dr Sgroi said, Sophia felt that it was then her duty and destiny to take over that role, thereby protecting the rest of the family. She would also have believed that if she conformed to her father's threats in relation to not telling about the abuse, he would not kill her or hurt other family members. Dr Sgroi agreed with Mr Rogers when he said that this belief of Sophia's was clearly wrong. 'Paradoxically, it made her feel in control and rather more powerful,' she said. Dr Sgroi said that this kind of cognitive distortion about an abusive parent was very common, and that it was frequently accompanied by 'the false sense of being in control and powerful'. She said the cause was the 'incredibly violent environment' in which Sophia had grown up.

Dr Sgroi described dissociation as the underlying mechanism for elements which are the hallmarks of post-traumatic stress disorder. 'Unfortunately, although it is adaptive and helpful in the sense that it protects people when they are being seriously abused, it also very much cuts them off from information about everyday ordinary life events and I think can seriously impair a person's judgment.' Dr Sgroi stressed that she did not want to take away from Sophia's remarkable achievements by analysing her thought processes in this way. During lunch in one of the pubs along the quays of the Liffey, Dr Sgroi reassured Sophia on this. 'The way you dealt with it got you through a lot,' she said. 'It did not harm anyone else. Don't knock it.' Sophia was not about to. 'It was a brilliant survival technique in a bad situation. I saved myself until I could cope.'

Sophia's lawyers also called Dr Swann as an expert witness. Dr Swann said that while Sophia was a student, she would simply not have been capable of 'breaking the story' of her life. 'She had not even begun to address the issues that would have overwhelmed her if she had allowed them to come to the fore. She had post-traumatic stress disorder. She was dealing with the impact of it on her, on her concentration, on her ability to trust others and her ability to make decisions.'

Mr Rogers asked Dr Swann if Sophia's decision 'not to go after her father' between 1989 and 1990 when she was an adult and at college was wrong, right, or irrational. 'I would say it was the only decision she could have made at that time,' she replied.

Sophia herself told the court why she had not told anyone about her father while she was at college. 'I was very distraught as a person because of what had happened to me. My confidence was below zero. I was going through turmoil.' When it was put to her by Mr Rogers that she had none the less got an honours degree, she said, 'I kept my head for the degree. That was all I could do. That was the bit of dignity I had to get out of this.'

Looking back, Sophia feels that those people who wonder why, as an adult, she continued to live in her father's house until he threw her out, and why she did not report his crimes until 1993, should look at the powerlessness of her situation. 'I only knew what I had learned from my life up to that time,' she said. 'When I was growing up and going through my teenage years, what did I know? I hadn't talked to people. I didn't have anyone to educate me about my rights. All I had known was abuse in a home which was really a sort of military prison, and professionals who seemed to turn the other way. The Gardaí had brought my brother back to my father whenever he ran away. The social workers had never come near me even after Gerry said I had been sexually abused. I had no faith in the system. All I had were my few books and my plan to get a degree and then take the system on myself.'

Looking back, she has felt intense guilt about leaving her sisters and brother and her mother in Cloonacurra, while she lived in the relative safety of her grandparents' house in Ballinacarrow. 'I had to become like my grandmother, not saying anything in case someone at home got hurt over it. I remember giving Michelle a gold chain for her graduation and she said she wouldn't take it. I knew by the way she said it that he wouldn't let her take it. He knew that I was trying to get her confidence. He was trying to encourage her to turn against me.'

In March 1993, a Kilkenny farmer pleaded guilty to raping and assaulting his daughter over a period from 1976 to 1991. It was known as the Kilkenny Incest case, and it was the talk of the country. The man's daughter had been in and out of hospital with serious injuries, had given birth to his baby, and had seen social workers, public health nurses and doctors many times over the years. 'Obviously, I identified with her,' Sophia said. She remembers a law lecture at Sligo RTC on the implications of the case. 'The other students were all talking about how incredible it was that nobody knew, and that the girl did not tell,' she said. 'I was there just frozen to the spot. The students were saying the father should have got a far longer sentence, and the lecturer said that seven years was a long time, day in, day out, to spend in a cell.'

Out in Ballinacarrow, Sally drew McColgan's attention to reports on the case in the *Irish Press*. She does not recall his response. The then Minister for Health, Brendan Howlin, ordered a public inquiry into the Kilkenny incest case, which reported in May 1993. Val O'Kelly told me that she felt the Kilkenny case in a way prepared the ground for the breaking of the McColgan case. 'People were suddenly made aware that this type of thing was happening in Ireland. Before, they might have seen signs and turned a blind eye, because they didn't know how to deal with it. Now here was a horrific case out in the open,' she said. Mrs O'Kelly said that a woman had recently approached her in the supermarket and begun talking to her about the McColgans. 'She said she had worked in that area twenty years ago in the late seventies and that "We all knew what was going on,"' said Mrs O'Kelly.

Sally remembers that in the same month, not long before Sophia did her finals, Michelle told her that when Gerry came home from England in the summer, she was going to go back with him. She said she had to escape from her father. Sally said

Michelle told her that father was sexually abusing her. Pressed by her Granny, Michelle said that it was in the past, and that he had stopped some time previously. Sally said that, in retrospect, she had her doubts that it had stopped. 'I think she said that to save me from any shame and further worry,' she said, in her subsequent statement to Gardaí.

In June 1993, Sophia received her degree with second-class honours, grade one. She was on the borderline of getting a first. Against all the odds, she had achieved what she set out to do. 'I looked at the results posted up on the board and I realised I was there among the top people in the class,' she said. 'I went home to Granny's and told her and she was over the moon.' In the High Court in December 1997, John Rogers put it to Sophia that she had not intended to go to the Gardaí about her father. Sophia said that she had intended to go within a week of getting her degree. 'I was very happy to go in there as a professional person and compete with these people,' she told the court.

In the end, events overtook her. On the morning of 21 June 1993, she was in her grandparents' house in Ballinacarrow. The phone rang, and Sophia answered it. Sally remembers her coming into the kitchen a few minutes later in floods of tears. 'She said it was Mrs Feehily, saying that Michelle was there and she was very ill with a hurt back. Mrs Feehily said Michelle was saying it was her father who had done it,' said Sally. 'I told Sophia to ask Mrs Feehily to get a doctor.'

A few hours later there was another call. This time it was Gerry McCarthy, a social worker with the NWHB. He told Sophia that her sister was in his office and that she was alleging that her father had been physically and sexually abusing her. He told her that he had made an appointment for Michelle to go to Sligo Garda station for 10.00 the following morning. Then he put Michelle on the line. 'She was distraught and almost incoherent,' said Sophia. 'She said "I've done it, I've told. It's over." She also told me to watch out. My father had said that he was going to kill me.'

10

'A BOX TO WHICH I DIDN'T KNOW I HAD THE KEY'

Chaos, turmoil, uproar, terror. These are some of the words Sophia uses to describe the impact of Michelle's disclosure on the family. Strangely, the events which would follow, while they seemed at the time a crazy and panic-driven chase through unmapped places, afterwards look quite typical; typical, that is, of what happens in families which have been brutalised and terrorised by a domestic tyrant who is suddenly, definitively, exposed. 'When Michelle phoned me, she was crying so much, you couldn't make out a lot of what she was saying. I was certain sure that my father would sink a knife in me,' said Sophia. 'I had thought I would be in control of this, but I wasn't. It was a total nightmare.'

Michelle's friends, the Feehilys, brought her back to their house in Sligo after her distraught interview with the social worker at Markievicz House was over. It was there that Sophia and Michelle had their first, real talk about what their father had done to them. 'When Michelle told me her story, it was the same as what had happened to me,' said Sophia. 'I thought, "This can't be true." I fought with her for a while. We fought against each other.

I said, "Ah no, Michelle, how could he have had time to do all those things to you? It was me he did all those things to." Then I realised that it was particularly in the last two years she'd got the same abuse as me. I had known in my heart that when I was gone out of the house, he would descend on the next oldest. But he had got even more physically violent with her. He had almost killed her several times. I wouldn't believe her, but I did believe her. There were memories that came up at me like a blast out of hell. After we fought, we cried and cried. Our heads were splitting, we cried so much.'

Michelle could have died during her last night of abuse on the mountain. Her father had made her labour on the land all evening, and had then raped and battered her until a late hour in the small bedroom where he kept a pornographic photograph which he said reminded him of Sophia. On the way down the mountain, Michelle had to carry a flashlight to guide the motorbike. It was late, and he did not want people to notice them. He got angry with her, and rammed the bike into her back, throwing her onto the rough lane. Michelle was badly hurt. She was twenty-one years old, miserable to the core, and she felt she was going to die.

Two days later, she was allowed to go to the house of a school friend, Emily Feehily. The girls went shopping, and in the changing room of a boutique, Emily saw Michelle's bruises. 'What happened to you, Michelle?' she asked. Michelle broke down and started to tell. Mrs Feehily came home to find the girls in tears. She heard what Michelle had to say, and brought them for a run in the car to Lissadell House near Drumcliff to try to calm her. In the morning, she brought her to see Dr Jane Dorman in Sligo town. Dr Dorman phoned the social work department in Markievicz House. The night after, Michelle told the social worker, who told the Gardaí, Michelle was so terrified of her father coming after her that she

142

had Emily and her mother sleep in the room with her. She was still shaking with fear. They pushed a table against the door.

Michelle was thin and unwell. She had been told by Dr Moran that she had anorexia nervosa. Sally said simply, 'Michelle had stopped eating.' This new trauma made her very ill. McColgan's days, though, were numbered.

Joe McColgan had gone to the mountain the day Michelle broke down and shattered the long silence. It was Sophia who had to tell her mother. Patsy did not take it well. Her husband had imposed with an iron fist the old discipline of keeping his outrages hidden away. It was hard to throw it off. Now she was hearing about horrors she had not allowed herself even to imagine. 'I was shocked. I didn't want to believe it, but I did believe it,' Patsy told me. 'I was angry and very upset. I did also think about the disgrace. Sophia had only just got her degree. What would it do to her chances if all this came out? Then, being an old softie, I thought that maybe we could get him help. I was still thinking I could change him.'

On 22 June 1993, at 9.30 in the morning, Sophia rang Sligo Garda Station and asked the ban garda who was to take Michelle's statement at 10.00 to come instead to the Feehilys' house. 'I thought it would be better if they came in plain clothes to a house,' said Sophia. However, Michelle arrived as planned at the station and said she was willing to make a statement. Sophia arrived soon after her younger sister, in a very overwrought state. She told the Gardaí that Michelle was in no fit state to make a statement and that they were to stop interviewing her. Sophia's memory of that time has gaps. 'Everything was thrown into turmoil. I can't remember some of what happened. But I do remember that Michelle was in an awful state. She was crying and laughing and cursing my father and raging at the same time. I felt protective of her. I was glad she was telling, but I felt she was going to crack up if she kept on.'

Sophia was not at all confident about the course of action which she was entering into. 'I felt hostile to the social workers. Why hadn't they done anything before now?' And she was unsure about the Gardaí. 'All I could think of was the times they'd brought Gerry back. I wasn't sure that they were safe people to go to.' In the event, Sophia was to find the investigating Gardaí persistent and understanding. One of them told her long after the investigation was over and her father was convicted, 'We noticed that you had no trust in anybody. We were determined that we wouldn't give up.' They also put her in touch with Dorothy Morrissey of the Limerick Rape Crisis Centre, who was to become a stalwart in Sophia's life.

Bravely, though fearfully, Sophia sat down on 22 June 1993 and made her own statement. 'It was a terribly hard thing to do. I didn't think I could remember, but I could. It was as if it was all in a box to which I didn't know I had the key, but I did. All these awful things that he had done to me, to my sister and brothers and to my mother, were all there in my mind, and they just kept on pouring out. I cried a lot giving that statement. It went on for hours. I was there from ten in the morning till eight at night. They kept saying to me, "How do you remember dates?" I'd say, because this was before my First Holy Communion, or this was when I started at the Ursuline — all the events of my life had memories of abuse attached to them.'

The statement is a catalogue of horror, full of pain, disgust and terror. One nightmarish memory prompted another, and another and another. Beatings, rapes, cruelties of every imaginable kind. And more. They were only a sample. As she recorded in the statement: 'There was so much violence in the home that it seems to be too much to mention'. This, for Sophia, continues to be one of the tormenting legacies of her abused childhood, adolescence and young womanhood. 'The memories keep on returning. I feel that I could probably remember every day of my life, and every day had its violence.'

Later that day, Patsy McColgan came to the Garda station. Sophia confronted her mother with her statement.

> I was very cruel to her. I read my statement out and when I read the bits about the sex abuse I kept on saying, 'Do you hear that? Do you believe me now?' She was in a terrible state. She cried and cried. She had no idea it was as bad as it was. She kept saying, 'Oh Sophia, it can't have been that bad.' She felt so guilty, I think she nearly had a breakdown there and then. Months after that, I felt very guilty about how brutal I had been to her. But I wasn't really me that day. I was in a state of shock. I had opened the box and all these memories came swarming out. It was horrible. I have learned through counselling that you take out one memory at a time, look at it, and then put it back again. But for the statement they all had to come out together. I was completely devastated. Mammy and I were crying together really in grief at the reality of my statement.
>
> I felt very undermined by what was happening. I'd planned this for years, and now it had been turned on its head.

It was hectic in Sligo Garda Station — Gardaí were all too aware that not only were the crimes they were hearing about of the utmost gravity, but also McColgan had other children and was still at large.

'One of them went out with the first page of my statement and they read it,' said Sophia.

They were immediately ready to go on the attack. I felt intimidated. One of them took me aside and asked me what I thought they should do about my mother and the other children. I thought that was amazing, that they would ask me, an abused victim of my father's tyranny, what did I think. They gave me two options, that the family could be brought to a hostel in Galway, or they could go to Granny Sally's, with a forty-eight-hour Garda watch on the house.

I couldn't understand this. I was after making a statement about my whole life of abuse. I was overwhelmed by memories. All along, I'd imagined that once I made my statement they would go and arrest him. Now the Gardaí were saying this could take several years. I had no idea I was facing into years of waiting with him roaming around free. I said it would be better for them to go to Granny's.

When McColgan returned from the mountain to Cloonacurra, the Gardaí were waiting for him. He was informed that serious allegations had been made against him and given notice that a barring order was to be put in place.

⁂

Patsy and the children, Keith, Sophia and Michelle and the two younger children, moved into Sally and Michael's house for safety. Health Board social workers had come to the cottage at Cloonacurra to advise Patsy to get a barring order, and she had taken steps to do so. Sally said that, at the time, her daughter

Patsy was 'like a zombie'. The family was torn asunder with conflicting emotions. The idea that it would be better to kill McColgan was aired, and dismissed. Sophia phoned Gerry in the south of England, where he was living with his partner, Sandy, and their child. He said he would come to Ireland immediately.

Having made her statement, Sophia returned to Ballinacarrow. She was too terrified to sleep. The Gardaí had promised that a mobile patrol would keep watch on the house in Ballinacarrow, but in the early hours of the morning, Sophia heard an engine stop outside. She froze with horror and rushed to the phone to dial 999. 'I thought it was him come to kill me,' she said. 'He had always said he would, and I had no reason to doubt him — he'd done everything else. He'd said he would kill me with a knife.' When Gardaí arrived, they told her a van had simply broken down outside.

Hours later, there was a case conference in Markievicz House, the first such conference on the McColgan family in almost a decade. Val O'Kelly, who had taken over as senior social worker after Denis Duffy's retirement in 1990, gave a history of the Board's involvement with the family. Social workers and Gardaí attended. Afterwards, Detective Sergeant Al Farragher, Garda Marian Judge and Garda Theresa McCabe made the grim journey out to Ballinacarrow to launch their investigation.

They were met by Sophia. She informed them that she was now the family's spokesperson and that she would dictate the pace of the investigation. She said the family needed space. When they asked to speak to Michelle, Sophia said her sister was in bed reading a novel and was in no fit state to be interviewed. The Gardaí then asked for permission to search the land at Killerry for forensic evidence. At Sophia's insistence, Patsy McColgan refused to give permission. Detective Sergeant Farragher assured the family that their investigation would be confidential. Sophia retorted that she was educated and knew the law and that Gardaí had enough information on which to act. She said it would be up to her to decide when the family would speak again. Stunned, the Gardaí retreated. Their investigation of some of the most appalling crimes they had ever encountered was over before it had properly begun.

Two days later, on 25 June, Sophia and her mother went to Sligo Garda Station. Sophia made a second statement: 'I have come to Sligo Garda Station today with my mother to withdraw the statement I made . . . in relation to my father abusing me,' she said. 'Everything I said in that statement is true and I stand over it . . . I had always definitely intended to make this disclosure, so that nobody else would suffer the way that I had been treated . . . I wasn't sure that my mother would side with me . . . I was under duress — I was, I feel, in the role of a parent. I had to do something to protect my family . . . I felt that nobody had the power to do anything unless I made a statement about what had been going on in our family. My mother will now take out a barring order and the family will be safe. We hope to get enough money together to get a new home and make a fresh start . . . I'm glad it is all over. I couldn't live with the repercussions if all this came out.'

What was really going on was infinitely more complicated. The family had turned the tables on McColgan, but everyone was still in fear of their lives of him. They had seized control, but they feared that he would retaliate in his usual, terrifying way. He had retreated to the mountain house. There were terrible arguments among the victims about what should be done. 'Decisions have always been really difficult for me,' said Sophia. 'With my father, if you chose one thing it was wrong, and you were beaten, and if you chose the opposite you were beaten as well.' Now the jailer was gone — what were the prisoners to do?

During cross-examination in the High Court case, Sophia described the atmosphere in her family at this time: 'It was like a hurricane in our family . . . you have to understand. I couldn't cope. I was actually smoking cigarettes on the day I made my statement, and I've never smoked in my life. I couldn't find anything to relax me. I was as high as a kite.'

In the end, the solution the family planned was a desperate one. Gerry would take his father back to England with him. 'We were caught between the devil and the deep blue sea,' said Sophia. 'Which was worse — the devil my father or the deep blue sea of the unknown? We thought we'd get him to England so that we would be safe here in Ireland. We'd try to get him psychiatric help over there and we'd pay for it until we got our own end of things sorted out. We didn't know what to do really.' The way they saw it, it was themselves against the world, as usual. Having put their trust in the law by going to the Gardaí, they were now embarking on a secondary strategy which involved telling the very people they had turned to for help that they no longer needed it. 'What faith had we in the system?' asked Sophia, bleakly.

Sophia knows, looking back, that Sligo Gardaí saw her as an obstacle. 'I felt I was protecting my mother,' she said. 'And when I told them it would be up to us when we'd speak, and that they couldn't go and search the lands, it was all a cover really as well. I couldn't let them go up the mountain, because Gerry was up there holding my father until he could get him away. Gerry could handle him because he was physically able for him. He was no longer a boy. We felt that if the Gardaí found out about what we were doing, Gerry could be done for aiding and abetting a criminal. I know I looked bad. I know I was absurd really and a pain in the neck. But what else could I do? We were not safe while my father was around. He was so unpredictable. He was on the loose, and we had every reason to expect he would come and murder one of us. If the Gardaí couldn't take him away, we would have to do it ourselves.'

Sophia contributed most of the remains of her hard-earned savings to help fund the venture. The night before Gerry took their father to England, he installed the fugitive in a hotel on the main street of Claremorris in County Mayo. Astonishingly, Sophia decided to go there and confront him.

I was with Gerry and we were in the bar of the hotel. Gerry was physically very powerful. My Grandad had sent some holy medals for my father. My grandfather, Michael, always had this thing that everyone deserves forgiveness, no matter who they are or what they've done. He's a total saint.

There were a few things I wanted to say to my father. I never wanted to see his face again but there was one or two things I *had* to say to him. I felt afraid, but there were people around and Gerry was there. My father came down from his room. He had some pictures that Michelle had painted up on the mountain, and he was there showing them to us, and they were very good, but very horrific. They gave us an insight into our horrible life on the mountain. There was one of him, and it was strange, because he thought it was good, and in my mind he looked like a demon. I knew he was a demon and that was why she had painted it.

I told him I hated him for what he had done to us all our lives. I started to raise my voice. I said he was never, ever to come near us again. I never wanted to see his face again. I said he'd be put on drugs at whatever psychiatric unit he was sent to, and he'd get electric shock treatment as well;

that's what he used to say to us. I don't know how he took it. I didn't care. I said, 'You've got a lot of praying to do. You'll have to pray hard to make up for the damage you've done.' I told him he was damn lucky to be getting a chance to get out of the country, because the Gardaí were after him and only dying to get their hands on him. His face was very intense. I felt he was calculating something else. He was pathetic too. He cried. I think he felt sorry for himself. I had nightmares for weeks after it, but I felt I had somehow put him to rest.

Back in Ballinacarrow, there was, Sophia said, constant pandemonium. 'We were all crammed into a small house with Granny and Grandad and we were all stressed out. We were all very, very upset. Michelle was still ill. We were trying to figure out what to do. Michelle and I were sitting in the front room of my grandparents' for weeks. We sat in corners on the floor like we used to in the cottage. We wouldn't sit on chairs. We were so afraid. I remember having my head between my knees huddled up for comfort. Granny was trying to get me to come and have tea. She was distraught trying to look after us.'

In England, McColgan was, in Sally's words, 'playing puck'; in other words, behaving badly. 'He went around telling people lies about Gerry and he tried to get into religious cults. He tried to sell the land at home to buy his freedom,' said Sophia. 'He created a show of himself. Gerry couldn't keep control of him.' McColgan was also sending bizarre, self-pitying letters home to his wife. In the end, McColgan went to the British police and said Gerry and Keith, who had returned to England with their father, were IRA activists. 'There was a lot of trouble in Northern Ireland at the time, so this was taken very seriously,' said Sophia. 'The special crime squad came and pulled Gerry and Sandy's house asunder looking for arms. In the end, Gerry had to tell them the truth: that he had brought his father to England to stop him killing us.' Gerry told the British police that if they wanted to check his extraordinary story, they could contact detectives in Sligo.

Things could not go on in this way. A family meeting was organised, and Gerry and Sandy travelled to Ballinacarrow to be there. The decision the family reached was that they would allow Gardaí to resume the criminal investigation of their father. On 8 August 1993, Detective Sergeant Al Farragher met with Gerry and Sandy at Cloonacurra. They talked in Gerry's Land Rover. Gerry told them that his father had physically and sexually abused him from childhood until he had left home in his teens. He said he would make a statement. On 12 August, Detective Sergeant Farragher and Inspector Joseph Shelly drove to Sally and Michael's house, where they were told by the assembled family members that they were willing to make statements.

In the week that followed, Gardaí took statements from Sophia, Gerry, Patsy, Michelle, Keith, Sally and Michael, neighbours, teachers and social workers. The catalogue of perverted violent crime they accumulated sickened the officers. McColgan's reign of terror had lasted twenty years. Gardaí searched the house at Cloonacurra, and later Gerry and Michelle brought them to the mountain house at Killerry. They filled sacks with forensic evidence, including pornographic pictures, spermicidal cream, poitín, a pair of hob-nailed boots, a broken mirror and a blackthorn stick.

McColgan was still in England, but was tricked into returning to Ireland. At 11.00 a.m. on 17 September 1993, Dr Moran phoned Sligo Gardaí to say that McColgan had returned from England, had been in to see him, and would be coming to the

Garda station after he had spoken to his solicitor. At 3.14 p.m., accompanied by solicitor, Dermott McDermott, Joseph McColgan arrived at the station. McColgan was advised of his rights, and was told that Gardaí were investigating serious allegations of sexual abuse against him. 'What are the allegations?' he asked. Detective Sergeant Farragher started to read aloud from Sophia's statement. In Sophia's words, the past was revealed: the rape in Derreen Bog, the beatings at Cloonacurra, the rapes at Killerry. The statement was not in sequence. Sophia's memories had not come that way. When, several pages into it, Detective Farragher read out Sophia's description of how her father had smashed her nose, McColgan asked him to stop and read that bit again. After this was done, McColgan made his first comment. 'That's total lies,' he said.

11

'A NOTORIOUS
VILLAIN ALTOGETHER'

I n England, Joseph McColgan had got himself new teeth, a new
suit and a new interest in religion. Thus equipped, he returned
to Ireland during the summer of 1993. He was barred from
approaching Patsy and the family. He returned to his natural
habitat in the derelict old house on the mountain. He did not
share Sally's view of him as 'a notorious villain altogether', and
disported himself around Sligo like a returned gentleman. One
man remembered meeting him during an election canvas. 'When
I saw him, I couldn't believe it,' he said. 'By this time it was pretty
widely known what he had been accused of, and I certainly,
having known him a bit over the years, did not doubt that his
family had told the truth. He was all dressed up in a new suit, new
hat and new shoes. He came straight over to us and started
chatting to the candidate. He was very suave and sophisticated,
and totally overpowering.'

McColgan had not given up on trying to intimidate Patsy and
the children either. Patsy said that when he was in England, he had
got someone claiming to be a social worker from there to phone
her. 'This person told me what sort of a demon I was for putting

him out,' she said. Now, he was sending flowers and letters to the house, besieging the family and causing great distress. Patsy would later hand the letters over to Gardaí. 'Mammy wanted to burn the flowers, but Granda insisted they be brought down to the chapel,' said Sophia. She knew one of the girls who ran the florist's through which he had ordered his unwanted bouquets, and she asked her if she would mind not allowing him to send any more. When McColgan next turned up at the shop, the young woman told him she could not take his order. 'He started going on about how he'd be so depressed, he'd throw himself in the lake if she didn't help him in his mission,' said Sophia. 'She told him Lough Gill was just out the road and he could go and jump in it for all she cared.'

McColgan was also hassling his father-in-law. This was the man he had accused of usurping his parental rights, of turning his children against him, whom he had berated and blamed for years for all that was 'wrong' with his family. But McColgan was shameless. 'He used to come to the chapel at Ballinacarrow when Granda would be there seeing to his duties as sacristan,' said Sophia. 'He wanted Grandad to pass on messages and arrange for him to see us. Grandad told him very gently that it would be better to leave well alone. I think Grandad got him to say a few prayers too. My Grandad would never judge anyone. He would think that every person deserves forgiveness, but he would also think that they have to look for forgiveness.'

Even while McColgan was in England, Sophia had not lost her fear of him. 'I kept on thinking I saw him. One day I thought I saw him after mass at the cathedral in Sligo. I was so frightened I went to the Gardaí.' Now that he was back, the family was terrified. They knew that the flowers and letters did not indicate remorse and that he was completely unpredictable. Sophia remembers that one day a friend of hers, who knew of her family's fears, arrived at the house with a dagger. 'He had this dagger strapped to him for our protection. It was very good of him — but it shows you how crazy that time was. The whole thing was terribly scary really.'

When he came back from England, McColgan took to going to mass in Ballintogher, the nearest village to the mountain house at Killerry. A neighbour said that McColgan asked him one day if there was a toilet in the church. 'He said he wanted to do his hair,' he said. Many of the neighbours kept their distance. They knew now the reason why they had seen McColgan's flashlight on the dark mountain late at night. They understood that the cruelty they'd recognised in him was deep and ferocious. They did not shun him, but he was not welcomed into most of the homes in the area.

The collapse of the previously all-powerful Joe McColgan was a long drawn-out process. 'When he came back from England, he had dyed his hair some sort of funny colour, like a reddy blonde. It was ridiculous,' said Sophia. 'When he was in the Garda station and they started questioning him, he reached an all-time low. He was suicidal. He had always had a very strong need to be in control of us. I think he felt so bad about himself all his life that the only way he could make himself feel better was to inflict suffering and pain on us. His way of controlling himself was to exert his cruelty on us. When he was confronted with our statements, the act of being in control fell down at his feet. He had nothing to hold onto any more. The way he used to keep his head above water was by suppressing everybody else and keeping them in huge fear. The doors shut when he used physical violence. There was no way out of the hell-hole. Now he was faced with the monster that he was. He had no supports for the first time. The hair wouldn't help. The suit wouldn't help. He finally got a glimpse of the real Joe McColgan.

During the interviews which took place in Sligo Garda Station on 17 September 1993, McColgan sat with his arms folded, looking at the ground. He was restless, rubbing his shoes on the ground and moving around in the chair. He appeared uncomfortable and occasionally upset. Having said that Sophia's account of how he had fractured her nose was lies, he went on to say the same about her allegation that he had given Gerry a terrible beating. When the blackthorn stick was mentioned, he said, 'A blackthorn stick? Oh my God!' When the mock drowning at Rosses Point came up, he said, 'Oh Jesus!' When frogspawn was mentioned, he got restless, and when a violent incident upstairs in the cottage came up, he said there were no stairs in the cottage. There are, in fact, stairs to the attic room, in which he had tried to make Gerry and Sophia have intercourse.

Sophia had by this stage made three, long, detailed statements, containing multiple allegations. After all of these had been put to him, McColgan was told that there were written allegations as well from Gerry, Keith and Michelle. Asked by his solicitor if he wanted to hear these as well, McColgan replied, 'If they are the same style of filth, what is the point?'

The following day, McColgan came into the public office of Sligo Garda Station, claiming that he had left a parcel with apple tart in it at the station the previous day. He asked to speak to one of the Gardaí, and this was arranged. Later, he indicated that he would like to make a statement. He was crying, 'Nobody loves me or cares about me.' He said he wanted to talk to 'his own', meaning his family. He said his life was a 'screw up' and he did not know what to do. He was cautioned and later signed a statement in which he denied sexually or physically abusing his sons, but acknowledged having had sex with Sophia and Michelle. He wept and said, 'I have nothing left.' He asked Gardaí if they could arrange for him to see his wife, and that she be told that he had told the truth in his statement.

In fact, his statement is a study in denial. According to McColgan, everybody in the world was responsible for his actions, except himself. Appalling rapes were described as consensual sex. He blamed his wife, claiming that his 'domestic situation was very frustrating'. He blamed his parents-in-law. 'I knew that she [Sophia] was my daughter, but I did not have a fatherly bond with her because she was reared by her grandparents and they interfered with my parental rights,' he told Gardaí. He said things happened 'once or twice' and 'always by mutual consent'. He claimed that certain acts, which had in reality deeply traumatised his victims, had been their own idea. He denied everything against the two boys. McColgan then turned to his own past. He blamed his father for beating him, the Marist Brothers for psychologically abusing him, and a man on a tractor for sexually abusing him.

McColgan would later claim that he wanted to 'spare my two girls', and went on to say that he accepted full responsibility for all the allegations that both Sophia and Michelle had made. 'I will be pleading guilty to them in court,' he said. 'I feel ashamed and sorry for what I've done to those girls.' He said Gerry's allegations were 'completely out of context' and denied totally that he ever abused Keith. He protested when he discovered that his letters to Patsy had been handed to the Gardaí, describing it as underhand and below the belt. 'I would not have done it to her and you think she is a decent woman,' he said.

When Gardaí came to Patsy McColgan in September 1993 to pass on McColgan's request that she visit him, she did not know if she could face him, knowing what he had done. Her children would have supported her had she refused. 'Eventually she said she would go,' said Sophia. 'Gerry brought her in. She brought him a holy medal. He told her his legs were swollen and that he had got new teeth. When she was leaving, she said, "God bless." Afterwards she would say that it was like talking to a stranger.'

Sophia said she felt her mother pitied him at that time. 'In all trueness, he was someone she had loved once,' she said. 'You can imagine. She had fallen in love with this man, and he had been nice to her. He had given her a totally false idea of what he was. You couldn't see through the *plámás*. It is hard to see someone until they show their true face. And when that appeared, it wasn't a pretty picture at all. After she saw him in the Garda station that day, she was totally devastated. I got a glimpse of the heartbreak in her. She had been a beautiful girl, stunning to look at, and very gentle and quiet. He had taken everything. He hadn't even let her be a mother. He was a total wolf, disguised.'

McColgan continued at large. Sophia had a job in a children's clothes shop on O'Connell Street, Sligo's main thoroughfare, and more than once she froze as she glimpsed him marching past in his suit. He went back to England for a while, to some of his new-found religious friends, but returned. Three months after making his first statement, he made a second one, in which he admitted sexually abusing Gerry, and to breaking his arm with a shovel — the charge he had denied and got away with in 1981. He further admitted that he had been 'hot-headed' with his wife, had hit her 'a few times' with his fist and 'maybe lifted my boot to her once or twice'. His second statement concluded: 'I now fully accept all the allegations are true. I know I was very confused and quick-tempered and I am really sorry for what happened.'

As well as minimising the crimes he was admitting, and referring to 'what happened' rather than what he had done, McColgan had to add, for good measure: 'It was not me as a person: circumstances created the situations. I feel good that I have fully confessed to everything.' He tried to sign himself into the sex offenders programme run by the NWHB in Letterkenny, but was found to be arrogant, domineering and, above all, unrepentant. At 8.55 a.m. on 8 July 1994, Gardaí arrested Joseph McColgan on the mountain at Killerry. He was brought to Sligo Garda Station and charged with a litany of violent sexual offences. He was taken before Mr Justice Smithwick at Sligo District Court and was remanded.

After Sophia had made her first and second (retracting) statements to Gardaí in Sligo in 1993, the Gardaí had suggested she call Dorothy Morrissey of the Limerick Rape Crisis Centre, whose counselling skills they knew of through other cases. In an interview given to me for this book, at Sophia's request, Ms Morrissey said that what she noticed about Sophia was that her concern was always for the other members of the family. 'She hardly seemed aware of her own needs. They all came down to Limerick to see me in August 1993. It was a long journey for them and obviously it meant it wasn't practical for me to see them often. They weren't at all sure what they wanted to do. There was just so much pain there.' It was soon after this that the family made the statements which formed the body of the case against Joe McColgan.

'Dorothy was a wonderful support to us,' said Sophia. 'For the first time in my life, I found somebody who believed me and who understood.' Ms Morrissey said that, like many victims of rape and abuse, the McColgans suffered during the lengthy period between making their statements and the criminal trial.

They had taken this huge step and suddenly it was out of their hands and they didn't know what was going on. The Gardaí did their best, but their hands are tied. They are not able to keep people informed about the progress of a case.

That is one of the reasons why separate legal representation for victims is so important. People do feel a lot of ambivalence around the time of reporting. Retraction is common.

Sophia had got a new job as a laboratory technician and had moved to a town in County Mayo. But her life was dominated by the impending trial. She knew well that her father could not be counted on to plead guilty. On 16 February 1995, she, Gerry, Michelle, Keith and their mother, Patsy, took their places in Court Number One in Dublin's Four Courts. Dorothy Morrissey accompanied them. 'Even right before the case, barristers and solicitors were asking me what did I think, would he plead guilty,' said Sophia. 'I suppose I knew his mind better than anybody from studying it so hard over the years. But I didn't know.'

Senior Counsel for the prosecution, Anthony Kennedy, warned the jury that the evidence they were about to hear was of 'cruel and wicked abuse of the worst kind'. He said they were embarking on a very harrowing trial, and that the case was 'of exceptional obscenity', involving fifty-one charges of rape, buggery, sexual assault and indecent assault. He told the seven men and five women on the jury that they would find the evidence hard to stomach, but that they would have to face up to it. Mr Justice Vivion Lavan instructed the packed press bench that to protect the identity of the alleged victims, the accused was to be referred to only as a man from a western county. Thus did Joseph McColgan become known as 'The West of Ireland farmer'. He was being held on remand in Arbour Hill prison, where other inmates included the convicted man whose case Sally had brought to his attention, the father of the young woman known as the Kilkenny incest victim. The two men had a lot in common. They had both got away with everything, short

— just short — of murder. They had both terrorised their victims and scared off the professionals.

The West of Ireland farmer stood up in front of the family he had devastated and put them through one final, communal act of abuse. He denied everything. He pleaded not guilty to ten charges (relating to Gerry) between 1978 and 1983, four of buggery, one of indecent assault and five of assault. He pleaded not guilty to fifteen charges (relating to Sophia) between 1976 and 1991, seven rapes, two incidents of buggery, three indecent assaults and two assaults. He pleaded not guilty to twenty-six charges (relating to Michelle) between 1978 and 1993, nine of rape, one of buggery, two of indecent assault, twelve of sexual assaults, and two of assault.

In the hushed public gallery, Patsy sat with her children, Sophia, Gerry and Michelle, listening to the man who had ruined her life, the lives of her children and the lives of her parents over a period of nearly thirty years, deny that he had done wrong. 'I felt I wanted to die,' she remembers. 'It was mental agony. I think I was very near the edge. I could not believe that he would get up there and say he wasn't guilty and try to blame the girls for the things he did.' And yet, it was so typical. 'All through the years, he was so manipulative,' Patsy said. 'He made it out that it was he who was being persecuted.' The girls sobbed aloud with grief and disgust when the court heard McColgan's claim that they had consented to have sex with him.

Gerry's evidence appalled all who heard it. He spoke in a low, tearful voice, and broke down several times as he named, in front of his father, the tortures he had undergone. McColgan stood, impassive, in the dock, looking straight ahead through his glasses. He looked like a country bank manager. 'The family was very supportive of Gerry,' Ms Morrissey said. 'They gathered around him to comfort him when he needed it.'

There was a long, tense weekend to go through when the court was not in session. Sophia said it was hellish. 'I remember the O. J. Simpson trial was going on at the same time,' she said. The trial of the former American Football champion for the murder of his wife, Nicole, and her friend, was getting saturation coverage on television and the papers. It was into its third week when the McColgan case started. 'We did not know how long this would take, and we had seen what Gerry went through in the witness box,' said Sophia.

On Monday, 20 February, Val O'Kelly described her dealings with the family. She agreed with Defence Counsel Brendan Grehan B.L. that Dr Moran had examined Gerry in 1983 and found no evidence of sexual abuse. She also agreed that the Gardaí had not been informed of Gerry's allegations. Mrs Candon, the teacher from Coláiste Mhuire, told of how Gerry ran to her in 1983, and how she had brought him to the Gardaí, leading to his being taken into care. A neighbour of the McColgans described seeing Gerry, when he was about nine, coming running across the fields with blood on his head. He jumped, terrified into her husband's arms. Patsy McColgan had come for him later and persuaded him to go home with her. The neighbour said that she did not know McColgan well, but that he had seemed 'a nice enough, ordinary man'.

Sophia had gone into court that day ready to take the witness stand and give her evidence. 'I was not afraid,' she said. However, when the court resumed after lunch, Counsel for McColgan, Blaise O'Carroll, applied for an adjournment until the following day. On Tuesday, 21 February 1995, McColgan was re-arraigned. Twenty-six of the original fifty-one charges were put to him. To each he replied, like a response in some ecclesiastical ritual, 'Guilty and I'm sorry.' The rest of the charges were set aside. After the plea, a detective read McColgan's statements to the court. At the end of his final statement, McColgan had scrawled in his own awkward handwriting, 'I am sorry Patsy for what I have done, I love you and I will never give up on you.' It was a sickening message, and the family felt its hidden menace. Mr Justice Lavan remanded McColgan and requested victim impact reports, which provide a professional assessment of the damage inflicted by the convicted person.

At the end of a moving interview with Joe Duffy on RTE radio in early May 1995, Sophia, using an assumed name, described how she had kept going through the years. 'I would say it was the love I have, the very deep love I have for my mother and my grandparents and for my brothers and sisters,' she said. 'This love was unending really. It stopped me a few times from feeling that I had to end my life. The abuse was so horrific that at times it seemed that it would be easier to let my life slip away . . . it seemed to be a never-ending story.' Sophia also called for a public inquiry. 'I would like to see some justice come out of this case,' she said. 'I would like a lot of questions to be answered.' Duffy attempted to get the then Health Minister, Michael Noonan, to meet the McColgans. However, the meeting did not take place.

The radio programme was inundated with calls, ninety-nine per cent of them, according to Duffy, 'sympathetic and strong'. Callers, some of them people who had been abused themselves, wanted to know why adults didn't believe children, why they did not listen. They said that these sort of things were 'swept under the carpet'. One woman said she was 'numb with horror' at what the family had endured. Others were in tears. One very upset woman called for Mr Noonan to set up a public inquiry into how the social workers, doctors and other professionals could have failed to rescue the children. One man said angrily that the fact that McColgan had raped Sophia after mass said a lot about 'this holy country of ours'.

On 23 May, McColgan was sentenced to a total of 238 years in prison, including eighteen counts of twelve years' penal servitude for rape and buggery. It was the biggest cumulative total of sentences in Irish legal history. Mr Justice Lavan told McColgan, 'You have abused your sacred trust as a father' and that he had engaged in the most appalling abuse of his dominant position in relation to each of his victims. The judge said that McColgan had scarred his children for life. However, he directed that the sentences were to run concurrently, meaning that McColgan would serve twelve years in total. With remission, this means that McColgan is likely to be freed in the year 2004.

Sophia was in court. 'I wanted my father to know that I could face him, that I wanted to see justice at long last,' she said. 'I wanted him to know I was not afraid of him. I was, actually, terrified.' She sat, flanked by a woman Garda, and listened as Mr Justice Lavan described the after-effects of her father's abuse on her and on her siblings. He said that the reports showed that all of the victims had been deeply affected. Sophia, he read, had post-traumatic stress disorder, the condition which would become the subject of much dispute in the High Court two years later. Sophia's Counsel argued in 1997 that she had been so debilitated by the condition that she would have been incapable, firstly, of reporting her father's crimes and, secondly, of suing the health professionals any sooner than she did.

Sophia also heard clinical psychiatrist Dr James Behan describe her father as a man who had been severely beaten by his own father when he was a child, and who had been rejected by his father because of his dyslexia. He had been beaten for hours by his father while his mother watched. McColgan had also seen his father beating his mother. He had suffered a series of sexual abuses since he was about nine. He had wet himself with fear once when he saw a religious brother beating another child at national school. McColgan had told Dr Behan that at one point he was hungry and penniless on the streets of Dublin, and an RTE executive had picked him up, brought him home and buggered him. Dr Behan said that McColgan had no formal psychiatric illness, but had been handicapped mentally by parental abuse and lack of love. He had grown up believing that it was a father's right to abuse his family. Dr Behan concluded that it was a tragedy that McColgan's case had not been diagnosed at an early stage.

Blaise O'Carroll admitted that it was difficult to make a plea for mitigation, and that his client's conduct seemed to go against every norm known to civilised society. He was, Mr O'Carroll said, a very damaged human being. He added that it appeared that if there had been more active moves by health professionals early in the case, some of the suffering might have been avoided. McColgan, in a badly fitting grey suit with a green pinstripe, and a blue tie, was led away. The respectable front had been torn down. Before he left the court-room, he laughed, briefly, meaninglessly. As he walked out of the Four Courts, handcuffed to a Garda, he covered his face with his free hand as the press photographers scrambled to capture the face of the 'notorious villain'.

That evening, Gerry, acting as spokesman for the family, held a euphoric press conference in the Ormond Hotel on Dublin's quays. 'My father was under the assumption that he would walk from the court,' Gerry told reporters. 'I feel as if a ten-ton weight has been lifted from my shoulders. It is like being in jail and being set free. It is a great feeling.' Soon after her goal of getting her father 'sorted out' had been realised, Sophia told me that she wanted her life to 'go normal now'. However, first of all, she had to have the answer to one stark question: 'Why did nobody help us?'

12

'TRAPPED IN
A SYSTEM'

꙳❧❀☙꙳

A key feature of this [the McColgan] case is that from an early stage there were repeated disclosures of abuse to health care professionals. [Despite this] the children did not receive protection. They were trapped in a system that was not responsive to their needs until fourteen years later when the full extent of the abuse they endured was revealed in 1993.

(from the report of the Review Group Inquiry into the West of Ireland Farmer Case, 1998)

1. 'Dr Jekyll and Mr McColgan'

'Ireland's most evil Dad', 'Sex beast father', 'Monster'. These were some of the ways in which Joseph McColgan was described in the front-page headlines of the newspapers on 22 February 1995. During the trial, which ended with him changing his plea to guilty, he had presented himself, in his spectacles and suit, with all the appearance of respectability. A neighbour said in evidence that she had thought of McColgan as 'an ordinary, nice man'. He was violent, perverted and cruel to his wife and children over a period of more than twenty years, yet some people knew him as a gentleman. Gardaí, social workers, priests, doctors and solicitors deemed him a fit parent. The home his children describe as a military prison was not far from a village. So was this a case of Dr Jekyll and Mr McColgan? Did he manage to cover up his crimes so skilfully that nobody knew what was going on?

The appalling truth is that many people knew many things about Joseph McColgan's violence. There was ample evidence. Patsy often had black eyes and bruises. She asked the North Western Health Board in 1979 to take the children into care because her husband was violent. Over the years, the children had injuries ranging from split heads to fractured noses to broken arms, and when asked what had happened, would sometimes describe an accident and at other times say, 'My father hit me.'

Gerry ran away from home more than fifty times and told the people he ran to that his father had beaten him, and that his father was always beating someone in the house. The children were admitted to hospital with letters of referral which began, 'Please see this battered child . . .' In one two-month period, there were three visits to casualty, two by Keith and one by Gerry. In another two-month period there were two, one by Sophia and one by Gerry. In all, the children had 392 contacts with the North Western Health Board between 1977 and 1993. There were also about seventy visits to their GP, but it may be, as Dr Moran has said, that the children were never brought to him with injuries.

At various times over the years, the children told social workers and medics that they had been physically and sexually abused. Occasionally there were witnesses to beatings, there were frequent instances when ferocious verbal abuse was overheard, and the sight of the children doing heavy, physical labour was commonplace. Nobody except McColgan and his family of victims knew quite how bad it was, and this must not be forgotten, but there was plenty of evidence to suggest that it was bad.

So why was nothing done to stop McColgan? One woman recently told Val O'Kelly that, in the area, 'we all knew what was going on'. A priest told Patsy that it was her duty to stay with her husband even though she had told him that he beat her and her young children. A young woman who went to school with Sophia said that people knew about things like McColgan having fractured his daughter's nose and run over his son's legs with a tractor, but that he was still regarded as something of a gentleman in the area. A senior social worker said that bruising around a child's neck, which occurred less than two months after another child had an injured nose, was not a serious enough injury to bring to court. McColgan was brought to court accused of breaking an arm, but the case ended up being struck out.

Part of the concern of Dr Moran was of course that of keeping a family together. McColgan himself was fond of warning off anyone who attempted to criticise his behaviour or change it. 'This is a family matter,' he'd say. When threatened with the law, he would invoke his constitutional rights as a parent. Sophia's grandmother, Sally, used to be accused of interfering with McColgan's rights as a father if she tried to help her daughter or grandchildren in any way, and they would be violently punished for it. She said she did not want to be accused of 'interfering in a marriage'. Dr B. McDonagh, the Sligo Hospital paediatrician, wrote to a colleague in 1979 that matters might improve for the family if McColgan could 'get his confidence back' and if 'the in-laws can be kept out of the picture'.

Neighbours who saw the children and their mother engaged in hard labour in the fields said they did not like what they saw, but, 'you couldn't interfere'. McColgan was like a caricature patriarch, but he got away with it. People backed off. Feeling that there was nothing they could do, they ended up allowing him the authority he claimed over his family.

When a Health Board social worker brought Gerry to Dr Moran after the boy had alleged that his father was sexually abusing him, the doctor was clearly overwhelmed. He brought Joe McColgan and his wife up to his sitting room above the surgery and got them to swear on the Bible that there had been no such abuse. Afterwards, he told the review group, he was troubled. Having been asked by the Health Board to monitor the family, he consulted a priest.

It is clear that the society in which Sophia grew up was traditional and Catholic. She vaguely remembers the Pope's visit to Ireland in 1979. 'There was a huge fuss in the village and everybody was going to Knock,' she said. 'Granda was steward and he said it was a great honour for us that the Pope had come.' Pope John Paul told the people of Ireland to keep their traditional family values. 'It is true that the stability and sanctity of marriage are being threatened by new ideas and the aspirations of some,' he said. 'May Ireland always continue to give witness before the modern world to her traditional commitment to the sanctity and indissolubility of the marriage bond.' He said that Ireland should not succumb to 'the trends where a close knit family is seen as outdated'.[1] One health care worker who came into contact with the McColgans told me that a priest had taken her aside once in the early Eighties and had said to her, 'That's a very complicated family. I wouldn't get too involved if I was you.'

Sophia is a Catholic and respects her Church. However, she has sometimes felt that it did not help her in her hour of need. 'Sometimes I felt it clashed with our lives,' she said. 'I remember one Good Friday me and the other children were huddled down behind the septic tank, too terrified to go into the house. I remember thinking, "God, why can't you come down and get me out of this? Show me a miracle." Other times when I was on the back of the motorbike coming back from the mountain after my father had raped me, I would want Our Lady to appear and tell me what to do.' In the absence of miracles, she was at the mercy of a system which appeared indifferent and was certainly inept, and a society which respected her father's rights more than it respected hers.

2. Blaming the Victims

There are those, including many senior staff at the NWHB, and an expert witness who was to appear for the Board in the High Court proceedings, Harry Ferguson, who firmly state that the McColgan case has to be seen in the context of awareness of child abuse 'at that time'. As in the famous L. P. Hartley line, 'The past is a foreign country, they do things differently there.' After Sophia's High Court case ended, Dr Ferguson explained the decision by the NWHB not to accept liability. 'The tragedy is that the case spanned a period when awareness of serious physical and sexual abuse was only beginning to develop. Enormous emphasis was placed on gaining the co-operation of "inadequate" parents and attempting to "nurture" them into being good enough parents, primarily by working on their relationship.'[2] None the less, it is difficult not to feel uneasy at the defence offered by the NWHB and Dr Moran in the High Court damages case of 1997/98. The defendants argued that Sophia was 'statute barred' from suing, and the Board further claimed that there had been contributory negligence on her part. Patsy McColgan was brought to court under subpoena by the Board, and efforts were made to show that she could and should have put a stop to the abuse of her children.

No doubt this defence was grounded in sound legal advice and represented the best course open to Dr Moran and the Board. Yet the fact remains that the criminal trial and conviction of McColgan in 1995 exposed the extent of his horrific crimes against Sophia and others in the family. The victim impact report prepared at that time on Sophia showed that she was suffering from post-traumatic stress disorder. That sexually abused children may be unable to disclose abuse until well into their adulthood, and possibly not at all without intensive support, is well documented. That battered women are often unable to protect themselves or their children is also well documented.

It was an outrage which could be committed again. The Minister for Health, Mr Brian Cowen TD, was asked by Fine Gael TD Alan Shatter in the Dáil on 29 January 1998, to direct health boards not to invoke the statute of limitations in such cases, and

. . . if he will arrange for the holding of an independent inquiry into the manner in which the [McColgan] family was treated by the NWHB from 1979 to 1993, and that the terms of reference of any inquiry include a consideration of the legal strategy adopted by the Health Board in the court proceedings brought against it and the failure of the Department of Health in the period 1979 to 1993 to ensure that guidelines issued by it on child abuse comprehensively prescribed the appropriate steps to be taken by health boards in providing proper protection to children at risk.

The minister said that the NWHB was bound 'in accordance with normal practice by a clause which gives sole control and conduct of all claims to the insurer'. Mr Cowen said that, pending the publication of the report by the independent review group set up by the NWHB, it would not be appropriate to comment on the board's handling of the case.

Mr Shatter asked the minister if he regarded it as appropriate that 'if the health board fails to adequately comply with its obligations' and, as a result, children continue to be tortured and abused and the Health Board is subsequently sued, 'neither it nor the state is accountable for its failure'. He pointed out that if the strategy of invoking the statute had been successful in the McColgan case, 'the truth would never have been discovered that there was adequate information available to the health board as early as 1979 that would have facilitated the bringing of care proceedings under existing law'. Mr Cowen rejected Mr Shatter's assertion that he, as Health Minister, could 'override the health boards and ensure they do not abdicate their responsibilities to their insurers'. He conceded that it might be, in his view, inappropriate, and that 'from a layman's point of view, the strategy was objectionable'. However, his conclusion remained that: 'The reality is that sole control rests with the insurers.' The Irish Public Bodies Mutual Insurances covers all eight of Ireland's health boards. James Nugent SC has, since the McColgan case, published an article in the *Bar Review* calling for the statute of limitations to be reviewed in cases of adults who were sexually abused as children.[3]

The review group's terms were not, in fact, extended to include the High Court case, when, arguably, the NWHB turned its full attention for the first time to the McColgan family. Nor did it make full or extensive use of the information which emerged during the case, even though its work was suspended until the case was concluded. It therefore did not comment on the legal strategy or related matters.

While writing this book, I spoke to several senior NWHB personnel, and some of the workers who were involved, directly or indirectly, with the McColgan case. The former senior social worker, Denis Duffy, told me that he feels the Board did all it could within the legal and social culture of the time. He said he was appalled at what the McColgans had suffered as children, and that he was 'delighted they won' the High Court case. He added that, although times and practices have changed, he still believes that, 'the biggest penalty is to deprive a child of its parents'. He said that it was very difficult for children to accuse a parent in court.

A senior NWHB official described the many advances made by the Board in its provision of support and protection for vulnerable members of society. It is clear that much has been done to improve services, and this is acknowledged by the review group. However, the official's parting comment left me wondering had he really grasped the central issue of the role of Patsy McColgan in the family. 'What I can't understand,' he said, 'is how the mother could have watched all that happening to her kids and done nothing to stop it.'

Another worker who met Patsy McColgan saw it clearly. She remembered her feeling in the early Eighties when she met Patsy and Joseph McColgan. 'It was as if her whole being had been subsumed into her husband's,' she said. 'She did not have a will of her own. She took his part, fiercely, against the children. He seemed to have completely extinguished her maternal instinct.' Nor did Patsy act in her own interests — covering up for Joe McColgan did not stop him beating her, in Sophia's words, 'to a pulp'. Sophia uses words like 'zombie' and 'robot' to describe her mother while her father was head of the household. She also describes her mother in those days as being 'a hostage' and 'one of us'.

A study commissioned by Women's Aid in 1995[4] found that there were complex reasons why women do not leave violent partners. The authors found that 88% of women felt they had nowhere to go, 62% hoped their partner would change, 44% feared further violence and 36% felt there was not enough support from professional agencies. Asked for reasons why women do not report violence in the home to the police — and only about 20% do — 84% of women surveyed said they were afraid that their husband would take revenge, and 62% felt that it would do no good.

Patsy McColgan went to Sligo to seek help to leave her husband in 1979. She told social workers that her husband was violent and that the children were not safe. She was given legal advice, the gist of which she took to be that a barring order would have to be renewed in three months, and that a separation would be expensive.

'I didn't know my options,' said Patsy. 'Where do you go in Ireland with five children and no money? I had never claimed dole myself and I was brought up not to go into debt. I didn't know if I'd be entitled to anything. If you put yourself in my shoes, if you are an underdog, you can't hit back. You are brainwashed and you have no confidence in yourself. You've just no power at all.'

Patsy McColgan might have qualified for supplementary welfare allowances and other benefits. What Women's Aid stresses is that women seeking to leave violent men need time and support.

The Coolock Community Law Centre has recommended that a pro-prosecution policy on domestic violence should be adopted. 'Decisions to proceed with the prosecution, however, would rest with the prosecution, not the victim,' it suggests.[5] This would be in line with policy in parts of the United States, where it is recognised that women frequently withdraw complaints or refuse to give evidence against their partner for a variety of reasons, not least their fear of the consequences. Patsy McColgan was, in 1979, encouraged to seek reconciliation with her husband. When she went home, McColgan threatened her that if she ever tried to leave again, he would come after her and kill her.

Dr Liz Kelly of the Child and Woman Abuse Studies Unit at the University of North London has written extensively about the links between violence against women and violence against children. In a 1996 article,[6] she makes the point that domestic abuse and child abuse often occur concurrently, and that, indeed, even to witness the abuse of your mother is a form of emotional abuse. She goes on to say that 'careful attention must be paid to defining the perpetrator as the man who is abusing the woman; "the family" must not be so labelled'. Dr Kelly goes on to discuss the manipulation of mother/child relationships by the father/abuser, adding that insufficient research has been done on these issues. She points out, however, that recent British inquiries into child deaths have shown that the mothers of the children were also being abused and that social workers failed to address this in their response.

Dr Kelly cites a study of twenty women whose children had been sexually abused, and found that 85 per cent of the women had experienced domestic violence from the same man. Finally, she quotes from *Women and Children at Risk: a feminist perspective on child abuse* by Evan Stark and Anne Flitcraft, published in 1988. The authors found that 'battering is the most common context for child abuse and the battering male is the typical child abuser'. They go on to state that

> the child abuse establishment assigns responsibility for abuse to mothers regardless of who assaults the child . . . this can deepen a woman's resentment of her child and constrain her to behave in gender stereotyped ways that seriously increase her risk in a battering relationship.

The crucial point that the interests of the father are not necessarily those of the family is also made by Dr Elizabeth Stanko of the Institute of Criminology at the University of Cambridge.[7] Speaking at a 1995 conference on domestic violence, she cautioned against labelling families as 'dysfunctional':

> The evidence is far too overwhelming about how gender, power and control are exercised within families which themselves are nestled within institutions and structures which privilege men's control over women and children.

The NWHB did not know in 1979 that when Patsy McColgan went home she was told she'd be killed if she tried to escape again. This piece of information was revealed only in an interview for this book. Much of the literature referred to above was published after 1984, when the Board ceased to have any contact with the McColgans. However, it is available now, and should be read by those who still cannot understand why Patsy McColgan did not save her children.

3. 'I can tell you that it didn't happen.'

Essential, practical information and advice about domestic violence was available to health professionals in 1979 and thereafter. Women's Aid set up its first refuge in Dublin in 1974, and the AIMS family law group was writing reports from 1972. Social workers and others who came into contact with the McColgans repeatedly noted Joe McColgan's bullying attitude to women and children, and that his wife was very much under his thumb. They even noted that she was probably 'colluding' out of fear.

From the early Eighties on, guidelines and information became available without, it seems, the NWHB ever feeling that perhaps it ought to revisit the McColgan case. Val O'Kelly said that she had always felt that the case would present again (i.e. come to the attention of the health professionals). 'My only surprise was that it took so long,' she said. Mrs O'Kelly told me that when she was training as a social worker, sexual abuse of children was not part of the course. 'I spent four years at university and it wasn't mentioned at all. It wasn't in the knowledge. There was a vague thing called incest.' She would, in 1984, recognise that the McColgan family 'did present as having the characteristics of incest', and she would say so in her report of that year.

You have to realise though, the McColgan case was our first case and it was also our worst case. We did all we could, but we failed. I firmly believe after many years in social work that there are some families you can't succeed with and this was one of them. We did our best. The systems failed. The whole of society was in denial about child abuse at that time.

Kieran McGrath, editor of the *Irish Social Worker* magazine, agrees that there was little professional awareness about child abuse in the late Seventies and early Eighties.

I became a social worker in 1978 and first encountered child sex abuse in 1979. It involved two families living next door to each other and there was a big row going on between them. I went to a senior colleague and asked for advice. She said, 'What age is the child?' I told her the girl was nine. 'Well,' she said, 'I can tell you that it didn't happen. Research shows this only happens to precocious teenage girls. Don't you worry about it.' I said 'Fine.'

Mr McGrath said that there was an attitude which looked at incestuous families and said, '"Oh, that is just them." There was a belief system that if you tried to do something, it would only make it worse,' he said. 'The Irish Association of Social Workers held a seminar on incest in 1983 and the organisers assumed we'd have to bring someone in from outer space to talk about it.' The *Irish Social Worker* magazine published an article on incest the following year and social workers were invited to join an incest research and treatment group.[8] Mr McGrath said that things changed in the mid-Eighties, largely due to the efforts of feminist organisations like Women's Aid and the Rape Crisis Centres. The Rotunda's sexual assault unit under Dr Maire Woods opened in 1985.

Dorothy Morrissey, who was one of the founders of the Limerick Rape Crisis Centre in 1980, said that things have changed 'enormously' since then. 'People are more aware of services now and they are reporting more readily,' she said. Ms Morrissey said it was important that people should be 'empowered with information', and that separate legal representation for victims should be introduced, a view shared by the Dublin Rape Crisis Centre. Olive Braiden, its director, said that the great courage shown by Sophia McColgan was required of all victims of sexual violence who sought justice through the courts. 'The McColgan High Court case was unprecedented, and showed how helpful it is for victims to have their own legal team in our insensitive legal process.'

Ms Morrissey said she believed that the NWHB could have done more for the McColgans. However, she said that social workers in the case were 'up against inadequate law' and that the law continues to favour defendants. 'It is very hard to get a conviction on sexual offences,' she said, adding that attitudes have not necessarily entirely changed over the past twenty years. She cited the recent case of a woman in County Kerry who appeared to be treated in a hostile way by sections of the community after she had made a complaint of rape against a local man. 'The man was convicted in 1997 but she still faced the hostility and she had to leave the area,' said Ms Morrissey. 'You can't count on people taking your side.'

In 1995, after Joseph McColgan's conviction, Ms Braiden said that attitudes still needed to be changed. 'We must face up to the horror of child abuse. Attitudes towards families and the sacredness of the family will have to change if children are to be protected,' she told a reporter.[9]

Mr McGrath said that the McColgan case shared many features with the Kilkenny incest case. 'Many of the recommendations of the Kilkenny Incest Investigation have been implemented,' he said. 'But it was so far-reaching that if you did all of it you'd have a different sort of society. The hard questions tend to be avoided, because they are too politically hot.' He recalled that in 1986 there were those who opposed the Childcare Act because, they said, 'it would lead to the break-up of families'. One of the Kilkenny recommendations which has definitely proved too hot is the amendment of the Constitution to ensure 'the rights of born children'.[10]

In the North, awareness about incest was raised when, in 1978, Noreen Winchester, a teenage girl, was sentenced to seven years in prison for the manslaughter of her father. He had been raping her for years. An appeal court judge upheld the sentence, but, after a campaign by the women's movement, Ms Winchester was given the Royal Prerogative of Mercy. 'It was the force of public opinion that got her released,' said Mary Kaye Mullen, one of those who campaigned for Ms Winchester's release. 'In some small towns you'd get people saying things like, "Thank God, we've none of that about here." But you'd also get a lot of women coming up to you and saying, "I had to move out of home myself with my daughter."'

In 1986, Women's Aid opened a refuge in Belfast for women and children escaping incestuous men. Angela Courtney, regional management co-ordinator of the Northern Ireland Women's Aid Federation, said of the situation now, in 1998, that attitudes are changing about domestic violence and incest. However, she added, 'There are still levels of resistance, even among educated professionals, and despite report after report. In particular, people just don't understand the power of abusive relationships.'

One social worker said he was angered by the claim that nobody in Ireland knew anything about child abuse in the Seventies and Eighties. 'As a child growing up in the Sixties and Seventies I was at two Christian Brothers schools and we were all very aware of child abuse. We even had a vocabulary and we talked about it. You'd know which brothers were "steamers" or "queers", meaning they would touch you up or do other sexual things, so you tried to keep out of their way. Parents used to come into the school regularly over it. Social workers are still in denial about this. Until they recognise that, nothing can change.'

While Joe McColgan was being tried in the criminal courts in 1995, the Irish government was fending off questions about its handling of another case of a paedophile who had got away with decades of child abuse, Father Brendan Smyth. Smyth was protected by the Catholic Church at senior levels, and the Irish government failed to extradite him to Northern Ireland.

In 1981, three Irish children died of non-accidental injuries. In one case, the father of a child who had died had already served a prison sentence for an assault on another child in the family. Harry Ferguson has pointed out that the media response to these cases was low-key compared with the reaction in 1995 to the death of sixteen-year-old Kelly Fitzgerald, whose home had been visited by Western Health Board social workers, and whose parents were later convicted for neglect. Kelly Fitzgerald's case, like the Kilkenny case, has much in common with the McColgan case, not least the fact that the social workers involved feel that they did all they legally could. They told *The Sunday Tribune* after the controversial inquiry report came out with strong criticisms of the Western Health Board, that there was nothing they could have done which would have made any difference.[11]

However, the earlier deaths did not go entirely without comment. In 1982 in Dáil questions, Alan Shatter had raised the matter of health boards ignoring the Department of Health's guidelines. An RTE 'Today Tonight' documentary of that year also highlighted this problem. Mr Shatter said that his family law book of 1977 outlined clearly the steps that could be taken by boards to bring children at risk into care, including the use of wards of court proceedings to cover situations in which the 1908 Children's Act was deficient. The then Minister for Health, Fianna Fail's Michael Woods, undertook to provide clear legal information to the boards. Mr Shatter also asked Mr Woods to direct the boards to urgently review cases of children at risk in their area.

At the end of an interview for this book, Denis Duffy handed me a heavily marked photocopy of a page out of the 1980 Departmental guidelines:

The legal remedies for protecting children at risk are not entirely satisfactory. There are three relevant sections of this Act which deal with getting custody quickly of children at risk — Sections 12, 20 and 24. However, Sections 12 and 20 are concerned with cases where prosecutable offences have been committed against the child and the offenders are to be brought to court. However, in most cases of NAI [non-accidental injury] the

Director of Community Care will not be concerned with bringing prosecutions. The child at risk is usually a symptom of a family with problems requiring help and guidance rather than the invocation of the criminal law.

All this, Mr Duffy had underlined for me. He said that 'at that time' validation of NAI was seen as largely a medical issue, and that it appeared to him that social workers in general were not taken terribly seriously. When child sex abuse came up, he said, 'It was like the garden of Eden — we had not been there before.' The 1983 guidelines continued to stress that invoking the criminal law was something of a last resort.

On the page of the guidelines facing the one dealing with the law cited above, details were given of how to keep a list of children who had 'presented' with suspected NAIs. According to Dáil replies from 1982, the NWHB had such a list, though it may have operated in the Donegal community care area, rather than in Sligo-Leitrim, which had a separate administration. In 1978, Dr J. K. Heagney, the then Director of Community Care of Sligo-Leitrim, stated that he agreed with the 1977 guidelines, which also contained the guideline on keeping a list. Senior medical personnel also said the recommendations seemed to be working quite well. It is hard to understand then, why, from 1979 onwards, the McColgan children kept on turning up at casualty in Sligo General Hospital, getting treatment, and going home again without anyone noticing that there was a pattern and a serious problem in the family.

4. The Inquiry
On 25 February 1995, within days of the conviction of Joseph McColgan, the then Minister for Health, Fine Gael's Michael

Noonan TD, told *The Sunday Tribune* that he had no information suggesting that the North Western Health Board was at fault in its handling of the McColgan case.

> I have seen nothing yet which would suggest there's a need for an inquiry. But I am not untouched by the horror of the evidence in court and I will have enquiries made . . . We can all be prudent in retrospect but when you think of Ireland in 1983, there was no perception that these kind of things were happening in Irish society.[12]

Five days later, the Chief Executive Officer of the NWHB, Tom Daly, set up a review group headed by Michael Bruton, a management consultant, former social worker and former programme manager with the Western Health Board. Mr Bruton has taken part in a number of investigations into controversial child abuse cases, including the Madonna House inquiry. Madonna House, a residential care centre in County Dublin, was closed down in 1995 because of the sexual abuse of children by staff. The Madonna House inquiry report was, controversially, never published in full.

The group was 'to review the NWHB's involvement in the case and to assess the Board's response in the context of both the then current service and the likely level of response today, and to make recommendations to the CEO . . .' The other members of the group were Dr Sheila Ryan, Programme Manager with the North Eastern Health Board, who was a member of the team which prepared the report into the Kilkenny incest case, and Paul Harrison, head social worker with the Eastern Health Board. It was not a statutory inquiry and had no power to subpoena witnesses or take evidence on oath. Cian Ó Tighearnaigh, chief executive of the Irish Society for the Prevention of Cruelty to Children, was to the fore among those who said the review group was a totally inadequate response, and called for a full public inquiry. The review group was expected to report within a matter of months. However, it had still not completed its work when, in December 1995, the CEO asked for its suspension pending the outcome of the legal action which the McColgans had initiated.

After the High Court case ended, the group resumed its work, and the NWHB said it expected a final report within six weeks. The report was finally completed in July 1998 and published in August.[13] The report praised certain individual health workers for their efforts, but some of its conclusions were, unsurprisingly, strongly critical of the approach taken by the health professionals. It found that the NWHB had adopted a 'non-interventionist approach' and had not sufficiently looked into its legal options at key moments. Had it done so, it could have taken the McColgan children into care.

The report found that the Board, and the GP, Dr Moran, had emphasised the family rather than taking a 'child-centred approach'. It challenged the view that there was little awareness of non-accidental injury in the Board, but added that, 'genuine incredulity of sexual abuse existed in some quarters initially and may have persisted at senior social worker level and by Dr Moran'. It said that 'individual presentations to the services by each child were handled on an isolated and episodic basis . . . there was no systematic review of relationships within the overall family situation'.

There could be no comprehensive plan of action, it found, because 'the totality of information was never collated nor were necessary linkages made between hospital departments, community care and the GP developed'. No public health nurse records were available. The report found that the North Western Health Board failed to operate 'the structured operational response that was envisaged within the national guidelines existing at the time'. There was 'considerable misunderstanding about the role of the GP and this was compounded by the absence of any agreed monitoring or arrangements for feedback'.

'There appeared', the report said, 'to be an expectation that professionals would do what was expected of them without this being closely defined and a reliance on the assumption that the case would come back to everybody's notice if anything significant happened.' The report said that in 1981, the year McColgan broke his son Gerry's arm, 'undue reliance was placed on the Gardaí to address the Board's child protection responsibilities through criminal prosecution'. In 1979, 1981 and 1983, the Board decided against legal action without, it appears, taking legal advice. The review group said such advice should have been sought and that 'it would have been appropriate to have sought legal advice re a Fit Person's Order in 1981 based on the history of NAI in the family'.

While the report found that the initial two reports of non-accidental injury made by Dr Dunleavy were 'competently handled', it also found that the 'index of suspicion regarding possible child abuse was never raised by other departments, including casualty'. It highlighted a 'failure to convene, at key points, case conferences', and highlights the broken arm episode in 1981 as such a point, and the allegations of sex abuse in 1983 as another. It states that the failure to inform the Gardaí about the allegations of sex abuse was in clear contravention of the guidelines which require such notification in cases where it appears that the criminal law may have been breached. It draws separate attention to the apparent failure to hold a case conference in 1984 after Val O'Kelly's call for urgent action.

The report noted that, although Dr Moran did not find physical evidence of abuse, there should also have been 'an accurate investigative account' of the abuse, in light of the fact that the social worker believed the allegations. It found that non-accidental injury was handled well at first. It was 'initially very positive, gradually diminished and finally ended in an unplanned and unco-ordinated manner'.

It found that the 'operational child protection system fell down' between April and May 1984, when the strongly worded report made by Mrs O'Kelly was to be presented at a case conference which does not appear to have taken place. It found that the Board's solicitor was given an inadequate briefing by the senior social worker at that time. Declan Hegarty, the Board's solicitor, told the review group that when he met Val O'Kelly and Denis Duffy, he was only told about the most recent allegations of child sex abuse, and that 'no full history of previous involvement with the family including NAI was made available'. It concluded that, 'Comprehensive chronological information available on the family particularly in relation to the hospitalisation of the children was not presented or discussed in a way that evoked legal intervention. Had this been done, we believe a satisfactory solution would have been found.' Instead, Mr Hegarty had advised the Board that its evidence was 'entirely circumstantial and hearsay'. This meeting took place after Mrs O'Kelly had penned her report calling for either the father or the children to be removed from the home as a matter of urgency. The group describes this report as 'focused and insightful'. The review group said the children were 'effectively left at risk in a family with a known history of child abuse.'

The report identified training deficits and, while it said that 'there is now greater awareness in the Board', concluded that 'much work still needs to be done' to ensure the full implementation of the Childcare Act. It noted that the 1991 Act crucially underpins the Board's present-day response to suspected child abuse, particularly in relation to the availability of supervision orders, which give social workers the right of access to children. Denis Duffy told me that the absence of such a right prior to 1991 had been a key problem in the McColgan case, especially with regard to Sophia and the younger children.

The report found that on the crucial issue of co-ordinating information, the system in the Board remained underdeveloped. However, it commended the Board for putting in place a system of audit of child protection services, and for designating a senior social worker as the person to whom notifications of suspected child abuse are made. This worker has responsibility for ensuring that a 'care management plan' is put in place. It noted that a 'planned system of review of case conference decisions' now occurs, and that 'there is a system for keeping professional case files open even where cases are not deemed to be at risk'. The report found: 'It is our conclusion that the Board has made and is continuing to make strenuous and consistent efforts to effectively manage its childcare responsibilities.'

Sophia was the first of the McColgan children to end up in hospital, referred by Dr Dunleavy as a 'battered child' with a fractured nose, in 1979. Her mother asked for her to be put in care, and a place was reserved for her. However, soon afterwards, her father was advised to make his peace with his wife, and to go and see Sophia in hospital. The then senior social worker, Mr Duffy, told me that he thought McColgan should 'be making up to the child for his misdemeanour', but, when asked did McColgan acknowledge any misdemeanour, he replied, 'No way. He was as white as driven snow in his eyes.' It is hard to see, therefore, what was to be achieved from this proposal, and the visit was, in the event, a terrifying and ominous experience for Sophia.

Dr McDonagh told the case conference that followed that her injury was consistent with her story that her father had beaten her, but other causes could not be ruled out. Dr Dunleavy was not invited to the conference. 'A recourse to court proceedings would have been unlikely to succeed,' Mr Duffy told me, 'because of the legal situation and the culture of the time. To rush into court without sufficient evidence, and to lose a case would have placed the child in a more precarious position. Then McColgan could say he was proved innocent. The consequence of that doesn't bear thinking about. It would be a life sentence for the victims. You couldn't do that if you cared about kids.'

Before Sophia could return to Out-patients for a check-up, her brother Gerry was admitted to Casualty, again referred by Dr Dunleavy, and again as a 'battered child'. In 1981, after the Gardaí drew the Board's attention to the fact that Gerry had been treated in Sligo Hospital for a broken arm, and that he was now alleging that his father had broken it, enquiries were made within the Board, but Sophia's case was not reviewed.

In 1983, Gerry disclosed that Sophia had been sexually abused, and gave physical details to health workers. There was no immediate case conference, and nobody interviewed Sophia. Val O'Kelly told the Board that Sophia should be spoken to, but her own efforts to do that came to nothing. Mrs O'Kelly said she spoke to the headmistress of Sophia's school, but all she felt able to tell her was that Sophia might be under stress because of problems at home. Mrs O'Kelly told me that she had fears as to what might happen to Sophia if she approached her and the girl told her father. The review group accepted that there were, and remain, problems about interviewing children without their parents' consent. It suggested that a less stringent view of confidentiality than Val O'Kelly's might now be taken. Denis Duffy's view on confidentiality was certainly stringent: 'Confidentiality meant to social workers that any information they received almost fell within the seal of the confessional,' he said. Alan Shatter said that there would have been no impediment to the NWHB's telling Sophia's headmistress frankly what it knew and suspected about her home background. There is urgent need for these issues to be clarified by the Minister for Health.

Mr Duffy told me that the Health Board could not have helped Sophia, given what it knew and the powers it had. 'All we were acting on was suspicion,' he said. 'We could have offered voluntary care that wouldn't have been accepted. The McColgans accepted it for Gerry in 1983 because he was rocking the boat at home. But Sophia was suffering in total damn silence, the poor dear.'

And that was that. 'There was a lot of flurry and after that, nothing,' said Sophia. 'A big zero.'

---

1. Patrick Nolan, *The Irish Times*, 2 October 1979.

2. Harry Ferguson, *The Irish Times*, 26 January 1998.

3. James Nugent, *The Bar Review*, Vol. 3, Issue 5, pp 222 ff.

4. *Making the Links*, Kelleher and Associates and Monica O'Connor, Dublin, Women's Aid 1995, pp 22 and 23.

5. op. cit., p. 113.

6. Liz Kelly, 'When Woman Protection is the Best Kind of Child Protection: Children, Domestic Violence and Child Abuse', in *Administration*, Vol. 44, No. 2, Summer 1996, pp 123 ff.

7. Elizabeth Stanko, *Domestic Violence — the victim and the perpetrator*, Conference Report, St George's Mental Health Library, London 1995.

8. Ruth Torode, 'Incest Treatment and Research Group', in *Irish Social Worker*, Vol. 3, No. 3, pp 14–16, July 1984.

9. Stephen O'Brien, *The Irish Independent*, 4 March 1995, p. 4.

10. *Kilkenny Incest Investigation Report*, Government publications, Dublin 1993, p. 96.

11. Susan McKay, *The Sunday Tribune*, 5 May 1996, p. 6.

12. Susan McKay, *The Sunday Tribune*, 26 February 1995, p. 1.

13. *The West of Ireland Farmer Report* NWHB, 1998.

13

'HOW ARE YOU?'

On a winter evening in January 1998, Sophia and some of her family were in Bewley's café on Westmoreland Street in Dublin, after a long, gruelling day in the High Court. She was trying to explain to the Spanish waitress that she wanted red sauce for her chips, but the waitress couldn't understand. 'Just for a brief moment,' Sophia said, 'I looked up and this man was standing there and he said, in a very gentle, nice way, "How are you?"'

I looked at his face, and I looked into his eyes, and there was a twinkle in his eyes. For a brief moment in time, I felt as if somebody had embraced me. It was a beautiful warm feeling. I realised it was Brendan Kennelly, the poet and professor at Trinity College. I had seen him on 'The Late, Late Show' talking about women. He said on the programme that women were the be-all and end-all, the beginning and the end. He said he loved women, all kinds of women, though he still hadn't found the love of his life. So there he was in Bewley's, with his silvery hair, and this cheerful twinkle in his eyes and his lovely face when he smiled. And I thought to myself, here is the man who thinks he loves all kinds of women, and I thought, well I know he loved me there for a few seconds in time. 'How are you?' he said, and I said back to him, 'How are you?' As he walked away, I felt comforted.

I believe that a lot of the violence and cruelty in the world comes from men. There are a lot of violent men out there, men who are cruel to women and to children, and who think that women are only there to look after them. They treat women badly and they take women for granted. They think their children belong to them. In the past, men were very threatening to me, because of what my father did to me. However, I know too that there are good men, men who care for women and would never hurt anyone.

After the High Court case, Sophia's face was well known. As she and I walked along the main street of a small town in County Sligo, an elderly woman in a headscarf and raincoat stopped, put down her shopping bags and seized Sophia's hands. 'Is it Sophia?' she said, warmly. 'You were just wonderful. You are a brave, brave girl. God bless you.' Sophia thanked her.

Further up the street, an elderly nun in full habit stared, and then approached. 'Are you one of the McColgans?' she said.

'Yes,' said Sophia.

'Which one?'

'Sophia.'

The nun gasped. 'Well, you know, it was terrible what happened. But you have to put the past behind you and forget about it. Don't mind about counselling. It'll only remind you about things best forgotten. Don't look behind you.'

Sophia thanked the nun for her advice. But she is not going to take it. 'The one thing I hate to hear is "leave it behind you". A lot of people who say it mean well by it, although some of them are the very ones who'd have advised me that there was nothing I could do about my father, and there was nothing I could do about the professionals who let me down. A lot of victims try to put it behind them. They hide it away. That way it does them harm. It is like the skeleton in the closet — what happens when someone opens the door?'

'I don't know where I would have been without my counsellors. First of all Dorothy Morrissey of the Limerick Rape Crisis Centre, whom we all went to see in 1993. She was the first person who really believed me and understood; then Ruth McNeely from the Mayo Rape Crisis Centre, who has helped me so much. Through her I have learned to face my past, deal with it, and put it in the proper perspective. The women I have met in the Rape Crisis Centres have taught me skills to lead a normal life — more normal than most people. I don't worry about trivial things. Sabina Christensen, the psychologist, has also given me great help and understanding.'

The counsellors who have worked with Sophia speak warmly of her. Ms McNeely said that Sophia had grown up never seeing an adult effectively stand up to her father, even those adults whose job it was to do so.

This is the experience of many incest survivors who contact Rape Crisis Centres. They have survived because they have found their own unique way to do so. Some survivors do not make it. They choose ways which ultimately destroy them, or they get lost while waiting. Sophia waited for the right moment and she waited a very long time. Her story is a testament to her will to survive, to her deep spirit and, somewhere in the absolute deprivation of her childhood, to her belief in herself and her truth.

Ms Christensen describes Sophia as,

A remarkable individual of great strength and determination, who not only survived horrendous abuse, but also sought for its wrongness to be addressed. She represented her family in the court case and she has also given a voice to other survivors of child sex abuse. She has proved against all the odds that sexual abuse can be survived and in her case, survived heroically. I have learned a great deal from her.

In August 1998 Sophia won the Junior Chambers Outstanding Young Person of the World Award. She had been nominated by Sligo's Junior Chamber 'for taking on and beating the system' and had already won the Outstanding Young Person of the Year for Ireland. The Junior Chamber is a leadership training organisation. Previous winners of its world award include John F. Kennedy.

There is one idea that Sophia cannot bear, and that is that 'The Family' must be kept together no matter what. 'How can it possibly be right to keep a family together in which there is constant abuse?' she said. 'There is so much secrecy and shame in families in this country. So many people know that there is a problem in their family about abuse, but they would rather ignore it and keep the silence than face it and rescue the children. They say to themselves, 'We can't let it out that this happened in *our* family — what would people think?'

Sophia said that some members of her extended family have shunned her since the criminal trial of her father. 'In the area where we had lived, I got a bit of harassment. But how would people understand? It was so horrific. It was as if there was a pornography studio up the road. But it wasn't our fault. We did nothing to deserve what was done to us. My father ruined our lives, and the lives of other people around us too. My Granny, Sally, and Grandad, Michael, were part of his circle of abuse — they could do nothing to help us.'

The torrent of Joseph McColgan's violence has irrevocably changed the course of the lives through which it crashed over the many years when he was the 'head of the family'. Patsy McColgan said that her greatest regret was going back to her husband in 1979. 'I do feel very guilty about that,' she said. Sophia, though, insists that she does not blame her mother. 'Priests, doctors, social workers, solicitors — none of them saw through and stopped my father. Who do you turn to in structured, civilised Ireland?' she said. Patsy said she wonders if her former husband (she has obtained a legal separation) would have got away with so much if his family did not have social standing in Sligo.

Patsy said that when she now hears younger women talking about no-good men, she has no hesitation in telling the women to leave. 'I say, "Leave him, run a mile. If you don't, that is the rock you will perish on". I stayed and tried to understand *why* he was the way he was, and that was a waste of time. I thought I could change him. I thought things would improve. I feel I wasted my life.' However, she has a home of her own now, a happy, peaceful home, and she takes heart from the relationships that have started to grow between her and her children.

'I would hope the kids wouldn't feel bitter against me,' she said. 'I did my best. I gave as much love as I was allowed to give them, if I can say that. What makes me happy is that they leave their kids with me. They trust me with the little ones. They don't see me as some kind of monster.'

Sophia thinks there is a lot of hypocrisy about how much better things are now, compared with 'back then', when she and her family were abused. 'The Rape Crisis Centres are doing a fantastic job, but they need more money. Social workers and some health professionals need to learn the psychology of families in which there is abuse, and how to look after victims. There are cycles of abuse — someone in a family has to break out. We really haven't a clue in this country about counselling. It isn't just the immediate victims who need it. The whole society needs help in coming to terms with this. It is a process that has hardly even started. Our father's abuse of us was stopped only a few years ago, not centuries or even decades ago. There is still far too much of the "leave it behind" attitude. This country has to wake up.' Sophia's words echo across the years what Anne Lovett used to shout in the main street of Granard, Co. Longford. 'Wake up, Granard!' she'd shout. Schoolgirl Anne Lovett died, aged sixteen, giving birth in a grotto in 1984. Nobody had acknowledged that she was pregnant. Neighbours and others told reporter Nell McCafferty that they wouldn't talk to her — if she wanted to know more, she'd have to 'ask the family'.[1]

Violence has not hardened Sophia. She said that after the Dunblane massacre in Scotland in 1996, where nineteen children and a teacher were killed by a gunman who then shot himself, she cried for weeks. The spate of murders of women in Ireland, many of them by a husband or partner, has a particular resonance for her. She said that she hoped that people would learn from her story, but wants her life from now on to be private. She said she enjoys her friendships, likes to have fun, drink a glass of wine. She delights in her child. Perhaps, she feels, when Gavin is old enough, he will be able to read this book and know what his mother came through.

'I will never, ever be able to forget the pain,' Sophia said. 'That is the sad thing. I cannot change history. I cannot undo all the things that my father did to me, and to my family. Sometimes I walk by the river and I watch the wind rippling the water. I'm alone and I face the bleak reality of what happened to me. I had to fight for my freedom. I used to put myself down. But now I see that I <u>was</u> remarkable. I <u>was</u> inspired. I achieved what I set out to achieve. I love life. I have met wonderful people. I am looking forward, and there is a strong light at the end of the road.'

Sophia identifies strongly with the courageous actor Christopher Reeve who, having become famous for his acrobatic abilities as 'Superman', was paralysed in a horse riding accident in 1995. Reeve wrote in his 1998 autobiography that, whereas he used to promote the 'glib version' of what a hero is, that is, 'someone who commits a courageous act without considering the consequences', he now defines a hero as 'an ordinary individual who finds the strength to persevere and endure in spite of overwhelming obstacles'.[2] Undoubtedly, he would recognise and salute the heroism of Sophia McColgan.

When the victims of cruelty at Goldenbridge and other orphanages spoke out, the authorities said, 'That was back then, things are different now.' The same has been said by the Catholic Church about clerical sex abuse and its practice of covering the tracks of abusive priests. But if things are different now, they are not different enough to ensure that our children are safe. In 1997 the United Nations Committee on the Rights of Children slated Ireland on multiple grounds. In 1998, our biggest health board has its longest ever social worker waiting lists for families in which there is suspected child abuse. Kieran McGrath said that many social workers are currently involved with families with similar characteristics and dynamics to the McColgan family.

Refuges for women and children who have been abused are frequently overcrowded. There is a long list of rape and sexual violence cases waiting to come before the courts. Can we yet say that Ireland's dark ages have ended?

Sophia's story, the story of a child who grew up in the prison of her family, with her brutal father as her jailer, is horrifying. It is all the more so because Joseph McColgan's grim little regime was toppled only in 1993, by his children. Had they not, at the end of their endurance, somehow found the remarkable strength to do that, there is no reason to believe his reign of terror would have been interrupted.

'I really do not know why we survived. It is a miracle that no one died in my family,' said Sophia. No longer a victim, she does not want to shape her life around being a survivor either. She is quite happy with being designated by a newspaper as a crusader for survivors, but she does not want her whole life to be dominated by what happened to her childhood. She wants to study more, broaden her horizons. 'I was a long time struggling for my freedom,' she said. 'Now my life is in front of me.'

---

1. Nell McCafferty, 'The Death of Anne Lovett' from *The Best of Nell*, Dublin: Attic Press 1984, p. 48.
2. Christopher Reeve, *Still Me*, London: Century 1998, p. 273.